MW01235211

"*Janet Fouts kno* *new success for a* ..... *wrapped in a bow, in easy-to-consume ideas. Her book gives us hew gears for a new system. Pick this up and learn.*"
Chris Brogan, Co-author of Trust Agents

"*In a sea of shameless promoters and so-called social media experts, Janet Fouts is the real deal. From her love for all things digital to her vast knowledge of today's bleeding-edge social media tools and technologies, Janet is that rare professional who not only 'gets it,' but who shares her expertise in easy, accessible, human ways.*"
Sarah Brown, aka The Guru of New, Author of 'How Not To Be An E-Hole'

"*Janet is knowledgeable and practical in her delivery of real-world solutions to issues businesses face in online marketing and customer relations with social media*"
Chuck Hester Author of 'Linking In To Pay It Forward'

"*Janet explains the nuts and bolts of Social Media in a way that makes it easy for people to understand, and then apply to their business.*"
Kristie Wells, Founder and President, Social Media Club

Social Media Success!

Practical Advice and Real-world Examples for Social Media Engagement

By Janet Fouts
Foreword by Aaron Strout

20660 Stevens Creek Blvd., Suite 210
Cupertino, CA 95014

Copyright © 2009 by Janet Fouts

First Printing: October 2009
Paperback ISBN: 978-1-60005-164-7 (1-60005-164-2)
Place of Publication: Silicon Valley, California, USA
Paperback Library of Congress Number: 2009938533

eBook ISBN: 978-1-60005-165-4 (1-60005-165-0)

Trademarks

Warning and Disclaimer

Dedication

There's no way I would have ever even started this project, much less completed it, without the support of my family. CJ and Mike, thank you for all the support, encouragement and patience you had while I obsessed over what to say and how to make the book really useful. Your encouragement, support and feedback were essential to me getting off my butt and writing this all down.

Acknowledgments

First, I'd like to thank my clients. You let me into your businesses and shared your secrets, your problems and your successes. Some of you will see yourselves represented here in many ways. Our learning experiences together over the years are the source of this book, and your input as the book developed helped me understand the questions and find the answers. Thanks for letting me experiment on you!

Thanks as well to the valiant team of coders, designers and writers at Tatu Digital Media. You guys made it all look so easy and allow me the time and energy to learn, explore and expand our potential.

It's been an amazing experience working with such wonderfully talented people.

A huge thanks to my mentors in social media:

Aaron Strout, one of my first follows on Twitter who taught me to be a good Twittizen. He always answers questions and is quick with his replies; he's funny, informative and a great person to know.

Chris Brogan, who shares his insight and talent everywhere he goes. Chris doesn't pull his punches and from him I've learned a lot about how corporations can use social media.

Laura Fitton, for her 'go get it' attitude and unfailing humanity. She's the original queen of Twitter.

Chuck Hester, for showing me that LinkedIn is all about community and if you pay it forward you will always see your efforts and hard work return to you.

Megan Keene and Susan Tenby, for their unshakable enthusiasm for all things community, and especially Second Life, a place I'm still afraid to go to because I may never return.

Sarah Browne, the Guru of New, for teaching me something about branding and marketing with the big dogs...

Chris Heuer and Kristie Wells, founders of the Social Media Club who believe passionately in the power of community and pay it forward in everything they do.

Louis Gray for tipping us off again and again to new online tools and apps that develop as well as what goes on in the Silicon Valley. His FriendFeed stream is an indispensible part of any social media fanatic's toolkit.

I could go on and on. I've learned so much from people I interact with through many social media channels, too many to name here. I'm truly blessed to be part of an amazing movement where I've met fantastic people.

Special thanks to the team at Happy About who made it easy for me to get the work done, smoothed out any wrinkles that came up along the way and are truly a pleasure to work with.

Mitchell Levy—who liked what he read in my proposal even though it was just some thoughts pulled together.

Liz Tadman for gently but persistently moving the book forward and keeping us all on track and the wonderful editors who noticed but did not correct my slang and quirks so the book actually sounds like me!

Many thanks to Delia Colaco, who faithfully edited my words without changing the flavor and made suggestions that clarified and focused what I was trying to say. Working with an editor like this is a dream.

A Message from Happy About®

Thank you for your purchase of this Happy About book. It is available online at http://happyabout.info/social-media-success.php or at other online and physical bookstores.

- Please contact us for quantity discounts at sales@happyabout.info
- If you want to be informed by email of upcoming Happy About® books, please email bookupdate@happyabout.info

Happy About is interested in you if you are an author who would like to submit a non-fiction book proposal or a corporation that would like to have a book written for you. Please contact us by email editorial@happyabout.info or phone (1-408-257-3000).

Other Happy About books available include:

- 18 Rules of Community Engagement:
  http://www.happyabout.info/community-engagement.php
- I Need a Killer Press Release -- Now What???:
  http://happyabout.info/killer-press-release.php
- 42 Rules for Successful Collaboration:
  http://www.happyabout.info/42rules/successful-collaboration.php
- 42 Rules for Effective Connections:
  http://happyabout.info/42rules/effectiveconnections.php
- 42 Rules for 24-Hour Success on LinkedIn:
  http://happyabout.info/42rules/24hr-success-linkedin.php
- 42 Rules™ to Jumpstart Your Professional Success:
  http://happyabout.info/42rules/jumpstartprofessionalservices.php
- 42 Rules of Social Media for Small Business:
  http://happyabout.info/42rules/social-media-business.php
- I'm on LinkedIn -- Now What???:
  http://happyabout.info/linkedinhelp.php
- I'm on Facebook -- Now What???:
  http://happyabout.info/facebook.php
- Twitter Means Business:
  http://happyabout.info/twitter/tweet2success.php
- Rule #1: Stop Talking!:
  http://happyabout.info/listenerspress/stoptalking.php
- The Successful Introvert:
  http://happyabout.info/thesuccessfulintrovert.php

Contents

Contents

Foreword by Aaron Strout

As someone who embraced the concept of "social" in the offline world back in the late 90's, it shouldn't be hard to imagine my excitement over the explosion of social media in today's business, political and entertainment world. You can also understand how thrilled I was when my friend, Janet Fouts, sent me a direct message (similar to an email for those not familiar with Twitter) asking me if I'd write the foreword to her upcoming book. I haven't gone back to look at the time stamp on my reply, but I think it took me all of about 5 minutes to give her an emphatic "yes."

If you know anything about me, you'll understand that this was the perfect way to engage me. Given the number of times that Janet and I have chatted with one another online, she knew that this was the right approach.

This brings up an important point and that is the power of relationship building through social media. More importantly, it's the benefit of taking action on these unexpected requests—a phenomena many in the social world call serendipity—because these requests or connections can often lead one to places that could never have been anticipated. And more often than not, these unforeseen opportunities can lead to amazing results. Something that Janet well covers throughout the book.

In spite of the upside of social media, many large companies (and some small) are resisting these "unexpected" outcomes because the nature of business is to be organized. The corporate world abhors the unexpected, and works tirelessly to avoid surprises. This is due in part to the fact that in the past, maintaining a sense of control was the only way to create predictable outcomes. In a world where revenues, earnings and growth are king, this was the only way to do business.

The disruptive force known as social media is starting to change the rules and is creating an environment where one on one relationship building and value creation—two activities that are less formulaic and often can take a while to pay off—but activities that in the long run may pay off bigger and broader than traditional broadcast marketing.

Not only do I believe in this new way of doing business, but I've also experienced it on a personal and a professional level. From getting interviews with people like Craig Newmark, founder of Craigslist and Tim O'Reilly, CEO of O'Reilly Media (content creation) to getting coverage in publications like U.S. News and World Report (awareness), to driving partnerships and leads from Fortune 500 brands (sales). In every case, it's been a mix of hard work, creating the right relationships and then a little serendipity.

To that end, I'd be remiss if I didn't give you a little background on how I like to think about putting social media to work. Here are seven activities that I use myself and often share with companies thinking about getting started with social media:

1. **Listen** – What are your customers saying? Where are they saying it (think: Google Alerts, Radian6, Techrigy, BuzzGain)?
2. **Align** – What do you want to use social media for? Customer research? Sales? Product innovation? Make sure your social efforts align with your personal, professional or corporate goals.
3. **Include** – If you work for a big company, get the right stakeholders in place (corporate affairs, legal, customer service). They can help you guide and craft your social policy.
4. **Join** – Are your customers on Facebook? Twitter? Get Satisfaction? Sign up (but learn the etiquette first).
5. **Engage** – Talk to your customers, prospects, partners and even detractors. Ask their opinion. Tell them yours.

6. **Create** – Be sure to create lots of customer-centric content. And update it regularly.

7. **Measure** – Ignore this step at your peril. You may be doing a great job, but you'll never know if you don't measure.

The beauty of these "seven things," is that they can help drive new business, awareness and real return on investment for anyone. That includes individuals all the way up to some very large companies. Fortunately for Janet, I've decided to save the examples for her since she does a fantastic job of providing dozens of them throughout this book.

With that as a backdrop, what you'll also find out in this book is that social media is a transformational force that can impact all areas of your business including sales, marketing, HR, product innovation and market research to name just a few. I know this first hand because as I mentioned, I've experienced this power of connecting people and allowing them to improve, evolve and ultimately own the concepts that you put in front of them, but only when approached it the right way. Pitch your customers, prospects and partners and they'll run the other way.

One additional item to remember…social media is a slow waltz, not a frenetic boogie and it takes time for it to work. That shouldn't stop you from getting started immediately, but just make sure you read Janet's recommendations carefully and map the success stories to your business, organization or personal experience. Do that and who knows; maybe you'll have a smart person like Janet ask you to do the foreword to their book. And if they do, don't think twice because as they say, "what comes around goes around."

Aaron Strout
CMO, Powered Inc. (and dedicated husband and father of three)

Introduction

When I first started writing this book, it was a series of blog posts, some training manuals, emails, tutorials and notes I'd put together for my clients over the years. As I sorted through it all, I realized that I'd been answering some of these questions almost exactly the same way for 13 years! I decided it was time to write it all down somewhere it could be more easily shared.

It's not all old news by any means. Though we've been embedded in what is now known as social media for a long, long time, the tools have matured and new strategies been discovered. Some fizzled out and some gave fruit in amazing new ways, making it easier to connect with a large audience efficiently, without having to build the tools as we go.

Some of my co-workers and friends think it's pretty amusing (okay, maybe annoying) that I still get excited as new apps develop and new networks flourish, but it's a very exciting transition to be a part of. I get paid to learn something new every single day and then teach it to other people. How cool is that?

If you're reading this and expecting to get a magic pill that will bring in droves of business for you with a minimum amount of work on your part, or will acquire thousands of followers at the click of a link, put the book down and back away slowly. This book is not for you.

However, if you want to learn to understand how to communicate more effectively with your customers, your staff, and even your competitors through social media, read on.

Social media can do amazing things. It can create an environment where your friends and followers and even your own customers become evangelists and act as a virtual sales, support and marketing teams. It can help you spread word of your business, your products and your successes through extended networks of people you've never even met. It can allow you to create lasting and deep relationships across continents, religious and political beliefs in places you've always wanted to visit or never knew existed. It can open your eyes to the richness of human relationships and even find you a mate.

Social media success is not about numbers. It's about relationships. Build good strong relationships with your clients or clients to-be, establish trust, have real conversations, and your social media efforts will be successful.

1 What Is Social Media?

Simply put, social media is people engaged in conversation around a topic online. When you think about it, there are thousands of ways to engage with other people online and create either long-term or short-term relationships. Ebay, Amazon, Flickr, Twitter, IRC chat rooms, instant messaging clients, Facebook, Myspace, YouTube, blogs and forums are all examples of social media.

What social media **is not** is just as important a question. Social media **is not** a place where you can grandstand and push information out to the masses. The old "spray and pray" techniques of press releases, flyers and direct mail just don't work here.

Social media **is not** your traditional market research tool. People resent being inundated with surveys in traditional media; why would this be any different? Oh. Yeah. Because in social media they can fight back. They'll tell all their friends you've been spamming them with questions and marketing materials and you'll soon find they've turned a deaf ear and you're talking to yourself.

Social media **is not** a good place to pretend you're something you're not. Fakery is outed with glee in these circles, and the louder the better. Be as transparent as possible and you won't be singed.

History of Social Media

"Social media" may be the hottest craze right now, but it's really just a new title for a very old method of communicating. From the very earliest days of society, there has been a word of mouth method of communication that we used to make decisions. Where to find the best food, where it was safe to sleep at night, which vendors to trust and which ones to be careful of—we transmitted all of this by word of mouth, then print, then radio and TV and now through the Internets. Each method gets faster and allows you to reach further around the world, but it all boils down to communication and trusted relationships.

If you think about it, the Internet itself was created to be a social network. The web as we know it today was devised as a way for scientists to communicate over long distances. When RAND Paul Baran, of the RAND Corporation, figured out how to transfer data from one computer to the next (packet switching), ARPANET connected Universities at UCLA, Stanford, Utah and Santa Barbara in 1969. In 1979, Usenet was created and communication on the Internet took on a more social phase. Email and list-servs flourished and people began to form more diverse communities. By 1992, the World Wide Web was released by CERN, and by 1994, Pizza Hut was selling pizza through their website.

Since those early days, these tools have become more user-friendly and society has become comfortable with forming relationships through the Internet. People work from home and may never actually meet their employers face to face. They read blogs before they make a purchase and use crowd-sourcing to find the best products and deals online.

We are more likely to buy a product or service from someone we trust. If someone in our network reveals a reason to distrust a person or a company, we are going to be more careful dealing with him or her in the future. We may not buy products from someone we've heard negative comments about in our circle.

If you hear from a friend that the shoe manufacturer you were thinking of buying from uses child labor camps to produce them, are you going to think twice before giving your money to that company?

If you read a blog about another shoe company who donates a pair of shoes to a needy child for every pair you buy, will you not buy those instead?

"Harnessing the Power of Blogs," a research study of over 2,000 online consumers in the US, conducted by Jupiter Research (a Forrester research company) showed some interesting trends in online purchasing.

Blogs influence purchases: One-half (50%) of blog readers say they use blogs for purchase information.

The research path these users took was: read product reviews online (17%); seek more info on a product or service online (16%); visit the manufacturer or retailer website (16%).

If they used blogs to gather information for product decisions, 56% say they looked for a niche focus and topical expertise.

The Power of Social Media

There are legions of stories to show the power of social media as a force for good. Social good and marketing good. The two don't always go hand in hand, but it's nice when they do.

Grassroots fundraising on a personal level

David Armano had a fairly good-sized network to start with, and many of us have had brief conversations with him on Twitter, his blog or Facebook to name a few, and many in his network know him in person for business or casual friends. He has demonstrated himself as a person of character and honor and he rarely asks for favors from his network.

At some point he and his wife took in a friend who had escaped from domestic abuse with her three children, one of whom had special needs. Daniela had lost her home because she couldn't support the family, the house and the medical needs on her own on a housekeeper's wages. The whole family moved into David's tiny house while she sorted out what she was going to do.

One night David got an idea to see if his network could help Daniela raise just enough to get her on her feet and find an apartment. Nothing huge—just a place to re-start her life. Late that evening, David wrote a blog post with a picture of Daniela and the kids and reached out to his network with a simple and eloquent plea in a video to help Daniela. He posted a widget on his blog and asked people to donate whatever they could, no matter how small, to get her on her feet.

Within minutes (minutes!!) the news spread and bloggers around the world wrote posts asking their own networks to help with the widget to donate. Twitter caught fire with people tweeting the plea and linking to the blogs. Newspapers and magazines picked up the story and wrote about this one man's effort to help. The response was so moving that it still brings tears to my eyes. It did to Daniela's as well, and David chronicled her amazement at the outpouring of support, both financial and personal, that was the result of that one lonely blog post late at night. In just a few hours the donations through the widget topped $7,000. In the end people donated over $16,000 in financial aid as well as help with moving, furniture and a host of other things.

What's the lesson?

To quote Seth Godin, "If you've got a small, fixable problem, people will rush to help, because people like to be on the winning side, take credit and do something that worked.

If you've got a generational problem, something that is going to take herculean effort and even then probably won't pan out, we're going to move on in search of something smaller."

Daniela's problem was fixable. It was compelling, and it was personal.

Social Media Backlash

Social media is not all warm and fuzzy. It combines news and word of mouth in a way that can be exhilarating if it's working for you, and stunning if it's working against you.

Take the example of the "Motrin Moms' incident." Motrin put out a relatively innocent ad for parents using a style of baby carrier called a sling. The video intimated these slings can cause back and neck pain, and just what you need to relieve that pain is Motrin.

Personally I didn't find the ad offensive (yes, I'm a mom but I don't use a carrier), but some moms sure did. In the blink of an eye, mothers around the world roused their networks with their outrage. Within 3–4 hours the backlash was huge. The original video was posted on YouTube and backlash videos cropped up all over.

All this happened over a weekend, and all things considered, Johnson & Johnson responded pretty quickly, but the damage was done. The impact of this case was pretty interesting to watch, and it clearly demonstrated the power of the so-called "Mommy Bloggers."

Most of the storm took place on Twitter.

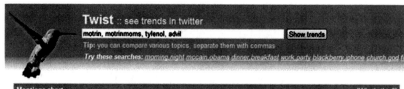

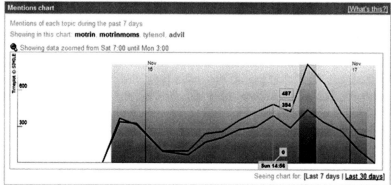

Image credit Jeremiah Owyang – Forrester Research

This graph shows the huge bump in traffic related to the Motrin and Motrinmoms keywords on Twitter. It merited its own hashtag on Twitter, forever to be known as #MotrinMoms.

Johnson & Johnson took down the video; in fact the entire website came down for a short while. Kathy Widmer, Vice President of Marketing for McNeil Consumer Healthcare, wrote an apology email and posted it on the Motrin website. Eventually, after a couple of weeks, things died down and Johnson & Johnson learned a valuable lesson: Even if you're not actively reaching out to your users in social media, you'd better be listening so you can put out the fire while it's small. Had they kept their head in the sand and ignored it, the storm would have eventually passed, but remember that these negative posts on blogs and in the news have a much longer shelf life. As of this writing (6/09) the Motrin Moms debate shows up as the 6th through 15th search results in a Google search for Motrin. How does that affect their sales long term? Time will tell.

What's the lesson?

The first line of action should be to get your ears on and listen to social media so you can see something before it gets too big to handle. If a storm blows up, be ready to act quickly and empower your staff to respond in a friendly and informal manner directly to the source of the issue in minutes, not days.

2 Quelling the Naysayers

There will be people in your company who pooh-pooh social media as a fad. They probably said the same thing about digital TV and smart-phones. Don't worry, you can find the data and case studies to show the naysayers they're full of it. I'll help.

The first thing to do is run some of those nifty tools I told you about and show them the numbers of people who are talking about your product, the company, or at the very least, the market you're in. Pull out some cherry conversations that are going on around your competitor and show them what they are missing.

For every client I have ever been called to serve, there has been at least one naysayer in the room. I go with data ready about the conversations being missed right now because they are at least listening. Gets 'em every time. There is no denying the simple fact that we are in an instant communication mode these days and people will, can, and do expect companies to be listening and responsive to their feedback online.

Statistics

For many naysayers, it's just plain ignorance about social media. They've made some assumptions based on the fact that their teenage kids are into social media networks and relate everything to that. Sometimes they've heard a few failure stories and relate them to all areas of social media. You need to show them the value and they may simply turn around. So get your data together before you pitch it.

Are you paying for pay-per-click advertising?

What's it costing you?

Could you replace some of that cost with a part- or full-time dedicated social media person?

Department Heads

Each department of an organization has different needs that can be served through social media. It helps to speak to their needs.

Make them comfortable by speaking in their language. Show them how you're going to solve their problems, not create new ones. Reduce their pain.

PR and Marketing

PR and Marketing wage epic battles over who is going to "own" your social media efforts. It's not impossible to get them to agree if you can divvy up the work and show them all that they will have their say and get to have a hand in influencing the way your company is perceived.

After all, messaging is their job and they've worked very hard to carefully craft your image, respond to questions and put a good face on things. They're not going to be able to control what is said about you out there. That's a given. But—and this is important—they can't do that NOW either. People are probably out there right now sending mixed messages about you and your company, and if somebody isn't listening and correcting misinformation, it becomes true as far as the public is concerned. After all, they read it on a blog, it MUST be true!

Show your PR and marketing team that you'll be making their jobs easier and more fun to boot. Show them the report you get from those first searches and listening tools so they know what's out there. Make sure they have a big part in the corporate social media policy development and that they are well versed in any of the tools you want used for the campaign.

Set them up with good PR tools and social media press releases and show them how it will streamline their workflow. Explain how you plan to measure the success of what you're doing, and make sure those metrics suit their needs too.

If you want to direct them to some leaders in the PR and marketing field, show them Brian Solis' blog at BrianSolis.com. He's principal at one of the leading PR agencies in the Silicon Valley (FutureWorks) and a leader in the push to promote new marketing and engagement through social media.

Then there's Todd Defren, principal of San Francisco PR Agency SHIFT Communications, who pioneered using new tools like social media press releases to take full advantage of all the benefits of tagging and rich media. Todd's been doing amazing things for clients ranging from H&R Block and Canadian Club, often thought to be traditional companies but who were willing to break out of the mold and dive into social media.

The PR folks often get short shrift as the "spin doctors" who twist what you do into something wonderful and cool that everybody wants. Some do and some don't. Some PR people have spent years developing and nurturing relationships with the press people who help them spread the word about what you do. They may have been using basically the same methods to communicate with those people for years, so why should they change it now?

Quite simply because times are changing. News and information are moving at dazzling speed and a carefully crafted press release can just plain take too long to pull together, distribute and follow up.

Let's just look at it literally. Standard practice is to gather resources to provide to a press contact so you're ready when they call. Then a draft press release is developed with contact information for PR to get those resources emailed or mailed to the contact. It's pretty much all text; it may or may not have an image or two in the release, with a link to an email address to request the image.

Some PR folks really want to force the contact to call or otherwise directly request information so they can re-enforce the relationship, fine tune the message being delivered and control what's being put out about the company. While this is understandable, it's SLOW. Too slow for today's world.

What if instead of a standard press release you sent out a social media ready release? There are download links to directly download useable movie clips or hi-res images. There are quotes and company info that can be easily cut and pasted into the article they are writing. Links to a bookmark list full of resources they can use to enrich their articles and blog posts down the road.

Remember that bloggers are becoming a force to be reckoned with and there are blogs for just about any sphere of interest. Bloggers typically don't respond well to press releases. Your PR person is going to need to develop a relationship with them through social media channels and if they ignore social media, they are missing out on major opportunities.

Once your PR people embrace social media press releases, have them think about blogging as the next step. Blogging is not a replacement for press releases in every case but it's a good way to extend the conversation started by a press release. Adding content to a blog in small, easy-to-digest bites is a less formal way to keep the connection established, boost search engine rankings and reach people who are beyond the press list.

"Social media is the primary driver of traffic to Ventureneer.com. Blogging and the social networking sites are responsible for 50% of our traffic—well over 100 visitors per day. My greatest success is that after launching only 2 ½ months ago our webinars for small business and non-profit leaders are attracting as many as 50 sign ups."
– Geri Stengel, Ventureneer

Ventureneer.com is a startup. They needed to build a following quickly and on a shoestring. Once Ms. Stengal knew she would be launching a new company, about 9 months in advance, she started aggressively building LinkedIn contacts, and she started blogging about 6 weeks before the launch of ventureneer.com's FREE webinars for small business and non-profit leaders. She distributed the RSS feed for the blog on LinkedIn and JustMeans (LinkedIn for the socially conscious), and Twitter a couple of weeks later and within two months had nearly 1500 followers and was #7 on topfollowfriday.com's #FollowFriday list.

Ventureneer regularly sends social media releases on PRWeb. They launched a viral survey about the resources small and non-profit leaders rely on and released the results for free. After just 2 ½ months, ventureneer.com was regularly visited by 100 people per day and 6 months later, the traffic was over 2,000 per day.

Well over half of Ventureneer's traffic has been generated through social media using the following vehicles:

- Blog (24%)

- Viral survey (10%)

- LinkedIn (10%)

- Twitter (5%)

- JustMeans (2%)

- Facebook (2%)

What's the lesson?

Social media as a communication tool is a fast and low-cost way to give your site launch a boost. Build traffic to your site and get opt ins through a little strategic planning and judicious use of social media press releases, blogs and micro blogs.

Sales

A good salesperson understands that building a referral network is key to getting leads. They also get that referrals don't always follow a logical route. One of the connections in their referral network maybe in a completely unrelated industry, but a connection of that connection's connection is a decision maker for a prospective client.

A good salesperson also gets how important it is to nurture the relationships with their connections with frequent conversations and other support.

Social media is an ideal way to nurture a large amount of connections and not only become the "go-to guy" within that network, but to support the people in the network by introducing them to each other and helping them promote their own products and services.

Once the sales staff understands this, they're going to see the value of social networking. All you'll need to do is get them the right tools and they'll be in.

If they still need a little convincing, find out who is in their referral network now. Show them who in their network is already using social media and who their competition is talking to. If the business space is fairly focused, there are going to be some crossovers in the networks and your salesperson will easily see opportunities she is missing. Help her find the tools and the networks she wants to be participating on, show her how to research for appropriate connections and she's on her way to social media success.

Recently I had a meeting with a top-ranked salesperson who wanted to understand what social media could do for his company. Now this guy is an old hand at sales and he told me most of his business leads came from referrals. He has a network of over 2,000 people that he carefully maintains with phone calls, emails, lunches, sales calls and sharing his connections to help the network thrive. He has spent 20 years developing his relationships and they've paid off quite well.

After 5 minutes he understood the power of social media. "OH, so it's a big referral network!" He got really excited, and we started bouncing ideas around. It was fun, and exactly why I love this job. Seeing somebody really "get it" and then being able to coach them through the ropes and watch them run with it is exciting—and I always learn something from them in the process.

Okay, but is social media a referral network? It can be. For someone who truly nurtures their relationships with contacts, social media is just that, the biggest referral network you could ask for. These seasoned salespeople work for years on their relationships with potential, current and even ex-clients because you never know where that referral is going to come from.

They send gifts on holidays and special occasions. They know when your kid is graduating, that your wife likes dark chocolate and you like Scotch (only Highland Single Malt). They also know this about your secretary, your partner and the competition, and they give every contact some personal attention on a regular basis to keep in touch.

Imagine the power social media can have in the skilled hands of a relationship builder like this! A good salesperson can be even faster to respond to events and news, cross reference his connections and make sure to introduce people to others they need to know to make their lives easier and better.

He can use the tools to listen to what's going on in the market and be the first to convey it to his connections, and to share the solution to a problem before they even know they have it. He can send less Scotch (I prefer Springbank 12 yr old, thank you) and spend more time in conversation.

Best of all, once he's got his listening tools set up and a strategy to engage, he'll have more time for sales.

CTO

One of the biggest pain points for the technology officer is when people come in with new hardware and software demands that will take up IT's time to support and maintain. Another huge pain point your CTO and her IT department have to deal with is the corporate culture of ignoring IT in the decision process. Common complaints I hear:

- It takes IT too long to vet the options

- They always want to use something else

- They won't support our decisions

- IT doesn't have the budget or bandwidth to deal with more

- They will shoot us down before we get started

As a web developer and a consultant, I encourage you to include your CTO in your decision making process. You might not know if other departments are considering a similar issue and solution. You might not know that IT has been carefully watching the networks and tools available and evaluating their options already. Give them a little credit and bring them in early to avoid having your own pain points later on in the process. Clearly define your goals, make lists of the tools you think you want to use (if you can do that easily), and then work with your IT department to find solutions you can all live with.

Help IT see they don't have to build anything and you're not bringing dangerous software into their network.

Although I'm a big proponent for self-hosted blogs, there's a lot to be said for getting a domain just for the blog itself. (More on this in the blogging section.) Beyond blogs and forums, you can get rolling in social media in existing online community platforms and take the load of supporting the platform and its users off IT's plate.

Human Resources

HR might have a few objections, depending on how tight the public policy guidelines are, if they see social media as the biggest time suck ever. You'll want to make sure that in your corporate guidelines for social media you've got something in there to cover how much time employees are allowed to spend online.

HR can find a lot of value in social media. Developing relationships with people working in the same space can result in positions being filled through the network, without ever having to post an ad. Sites like LinkedIn and VisualCV can help find candidates with the right skills before they even start looking for work.

Customer Service

The potential for social media and your customer service team is amazing. There are scores of examples of companies who have streamlined their customer service departments without off-shore out-sourcing using these tools.

Take the opportunity to listen to your customers. Social media can develop loyalty that you just can't get in any other way but face to face.

Point to well-known customer service success stories in social media like Comcast, Jet Blue, Southwest Airlines, Zappos, Whole Foods and many others as cases for social media customer service.

Social Media Is a Time Suck

This is a common complaint, and I have to agree that social media en-gagement can be a time suck, especially if people are not properly trained in efficiencies. That said, there are some arguments for social media actually saving time.

Let's assume you set aside time to go to one or two monthly networking meetings.

You leave directly from work, jump in your car and drive across town to the meeting place where you get a couple of pizza slices and a beer and re-connect with 4–5 connections you know and join in a conversation.

You move around the room a bit and meet 5–6 new people, collect their cards and chat about how you know someone who knows them, recommend a vendor and learn about a new process for something you've been meaning to find out about.

You listen to a presentation and learn something new and participate in a Q&A session afterwards.

You head for home after 3–4 hours, and spend a few minutes before bed writing down your notes on the backs of the cards you collected.

The next morning you scan the cards into your database, Google the ones you were interested in talking to again and find out more about their company.

With any luck you've got an hour or so in the morning to write follow-up emails and make calls to arrange meetings to talk some more.

Was this a successful networking event for you? Most would say yes. You got some new leads, learned something and maybe even defined yourself as a resource for people in your area of interest.

I'm not saying that personal, face-to-face connections aren't worth the time. Far from it. It's still important to connect face to face; if that's not possible, then by phone, Skype or video conference to really deeply connect. What I **am** saying is that you don't have to go through the long and often random effort of collecting business cards, filtering through them for the people you really want to connect with, only to set up more meetings to actually have a conversation. Many networking meetings have so many people at them that unless you've done careful research beforehand, you could get caught in the corner with the talkative guy with sweaty palms and bad breath who won't let you drop out of the conversation until he's done with you, and you never get to the people who truly interest you and who could really make a difference.

3 Inbound Marketing vs Outbound

Traditional marketing techniques tend to be "outbound." This means the message is pushed out to the potential customer in the hope they'll see the brilliance of your product or service and naturally come to you instead of your competitor. This kind of marketing can include trade shows and presentations, direct mail, phone book ads or circular advertising, blanketing the market with press releases and product announcements, email blasts to purchased lists, telemarketing, cold calling, seminars and banner ads on websites.

The average person in the US sees thousands of these outbound marketing hits per day in one form or another, and they're spending a lot of time and effort to block them out. They sign up for do not call lists, block email accounts, stop getting the phone book delivered, stop their junk mail, cancel catalogs and simply ignore banner ads.

With savvy customers who do all of the above, you've got to find a better way to engage them and bring them to your website or get them to make that important phone call for information.

Inbound marketing might also be called attraction marketing. The idea is to create lots of ways for the customer to find you and to get real information when they get there. Often the information itself is free. This could be a downloadable white paper, a blog post, an interactive customer service—anything that freely gives value without demanding anything in return.

It could also be a conversation had on a social network, or a customer service response to a plea for help on Twitter. The key is to add value without asking for anything in return, and to develop relationships before asking for a sale. Create a relationship with someone online and it eventually converts to something deeper. These contacts choose to do business with you because of the relationship, and when they need something they'll get in touch. They'll blog about you if appropriate, or tweet something about the product, and when someone in their network needs what you've got, guess where they'll refer them?

Inbound marketing may take a little bit longer to get the desired results, but unlike outbound marketing, inbound tends to build on itself. If you put a blog post online about a new approach to a problem that only your company has, it may attract attention. This attention leads to comments, links to the post and possibly references to the blog post on other sites or in the media.

All of this stays vital and alive online, and actively drives traffic to your site until it is taken down. People may come across it months later, but if the information is new to them and they share it with their networks, the discussion is renewed and you are rediscovered. This is a boon for search engine optimization as well. All those incoming links about the service you're offering from real people are more effective than paid ads on the same sites.

The goal with inbound marketing is to be a resource of information and enlightenment that your readers can't get elsewhere. Share industry insight and make yourself a resource for news and information.

This concept isn't at all new. Just go back to 1999 and read the Cluetrain Manifesto again. Read Seth Godin's book, 'Tribes.' Both are examples of thought leaders who really do get the way business is changing.

4 It's Not About You

I can't say this enough; if I'm repeating myself, so be it. Social media is not, will not and cannot be about you if you want to be successful. It's about building relationships, and in order to build those relationships, you have to give, give, give. Relationships are a two-way thing. If you give, they'll give and we'll all be better for it.

Any good salesperson will tell you that to really clinch a deal with potential clients you have to find the point that's causing them pain and show them you're the one to solve it. That's traditional sales and it works just fine. Of course, it helps if you can get them to listen to you in the first place, and that's where social media comes in.

Your main goal in social media should be to create relationships that endure and grow—relationships that expand your circle of friends and enrich the networks you join. To do that, you may look for ways to solve problems that come up in your network.

- Be a resource for people and they will naturally turn to you for information.

- Actively work to find solutions to other people's problems and share them without expecting anything in return.

- Follow up conversations about the information to deepen the relationship.

- Get to know the individuals in your network and offer them support, valuable information, links to resources and connect them with people you think may be interesting to them and they will do the same.

- Take the time to figure out what you can offer. Is it resources? Information? Connections? Entertainment?

- Be genuinely interested and people will be genuinely interested back.

It's not your fathers' business world anymore

Times are changing fast and the companies that can look ahead and see how to use inbound marketing will be a jump ahead of the competition who use traditional methods.

Naked Pizza is a relatively unknown "healthy" pizza chain in New Orleans that hopes to go national some day. People believe in the ideals of the company itself, and in fact, Mark Cuban, the self-made billionaire owner of the Dallas Mavericks, HDNet and search engine Icerocket, is an investor. Anyway, Naked Pizza started offering specials via its Twitter account. As a test of the promotion, they tracked sales for one day—April 23, 2009—and found their Twitter promotion was bringing in 15% of the register sales.

In fact, the promotion was so successful that Naked Pizza recently created an all-Twitter ordering system. They put up a billboard and replaced the words "call for delivery" with their Twitter address. Followers are rewarded with special offers and discounts. The staff of Naked Pizza does more than just broadcast discounts. They talk back to their customers and respond to questions asked on their Twitter account about the store and the idea behind healthy pizza on Twitter, their YouTube channel and Facebook.

In San Francisco and Los Angeles, @LetsbeFrank sells grass-fed beef hotdogs from trailers all over the city. Updates and special offers can be had on Twitter and Facebook.

In San Francisco, you'll often read tweets that @cremebruleecart and @magiccurrykart hang out in the same neighborhoods, and the @whatthepho mobile Vietnamese noodle cart can usually be found near ATT Park.

What's the Lesson?

Stop for just a moment and think about who your customers are. You may find they are online and ready to take advantage of social media to connect with you. I'm confidant that taking orders and tracking your favorite taco truck through social media is here to stay. In fact, I'm waiting for somebody to do GPS alerts that are messaged to your phone or Twitter account when the cupcake truck is within a certain radius. By the time this book comes out somebody may have already set it up!

C.J. Brasiel is a San Jose real estate broker who understands that re-lationship building is an important part of her business. According to a National Association of Realtors survey (2008), up to 50% of a realtor's new clients come from referrals. So doesn't it make sense to build a large and easily-managed referral network?

C.J. has profiles on LinkedIn, Twitter and Facebook where she nurtures her relationships with her clients (many of whom have become personal friends) and develops new relationships and connec-tions that not only lead to new sales prospects, but also to information that makes her a smarter realtor and businesswoman. She blogs for several real estate related sites and on her own blogs, TalktoCJ.com and GreenLivingSanJose.com, and a number of blogs for local neigh-borhoods. In addition, C.J. blogs on local and national websites where she gives sensible advice to home-buyers and sellers and discusses the local real estate market.

Answering questions from home-owners, buyers and other agents on nationally-recognized real estate forums like Trulia, RealSeekr, Active Rain and several others helped establish C.J. as a recognized expert in her field and gain perspective into what people really wanted to know about the real estate industry.

New clients frequently find her first on a social network, learn something from her, and call because they like the way she responds to questions and presents herself online. She gains their trust well before they send her an email or pick up the phone.

Twitter, it turns out, has been a good referral network with other real estate agents and brokers, and C.J. exchanges tips and tricks with Realtors from across the country, extending her relationships and referrals to out-of-state agents. Twitter also helps drive traffic to her websites and the websites she has constructed for her clients when she offers a home for sale.

C.J. reports that 30% of her current clients (not leads, clients) found her through social media channels. She rarely attends networking meetings in search of clients, advertises in the newspaper, or drops flyers on doorsteps. Her clients find her.

What's the lesson?

Connecting with your clients and potential clients as individuals first builds trust between you. Even if they are not making a purchase or interested in making a purchase, they may know or come to know someone who is. Just by being yourself, honest, helpful and knowledgeable, you can create a reputation that draws business to you. Sharing information freely, without asking for sales in return, is the key to inbound marketing.

5 Building Your Social Media Network

The whole MotrinMoms affair would have meant a lot less if the moms hadn't leveraged their own extended networks to reach as many people as they possibly could, as quickly as they could. In the old days, there would have been some protests, articles in the newspapers and on TV and then it would have faded away. Johnson & Johnson would have had days to assemble an action plan and react to put out the fire. Instead, the whole thing blew up in mere hours. How does this happen?

Let's say you've got a small group of 50 people who follow you on your blog, a forum with 100 members and a Twitter following of 500. So you've got 650 people in your personal social media circle.

On an average (according to Nielsen), each of these people will have 100 people in their own network, and each of their connections will also have an average of 100. Just this relatively small number of connections gives you the opportunity to connect with 6,500,000 people at just two levels of your network!

Of course, there will be some crossover, especially if you have a narrow business niche where everybody knows everybody else, but even if you only reach 2% of that potential market, you've reached 130,000 people. Amazing, isn't it?

It's easy to see why social networking is becoming so hot. The potential is outstanding. If your message is compelling people will distribute it for you with only the cost of the time it takes to send the message and nurture your network.

It's Not All About the Numbers

Sure, you have the potential to reach millions of people through your extended network, but HOW do you reach them and get them to take action?

First off, let me say that this is not simply a numbers game. There are lots of resources who promise to build your following automatically or on a paid basis. You have to believe me when I tell you that even if you have millions of people in the first level of your network, it doesn't do you any good if you don't engage them and create a real relationship. You have to at least know who they are, and better yet, engage them.

Sure, there are people out there involved in Multi-Level Marketing schemes (MLM) who believe that the more connections you have, the more opportunities for them to actually do something. But I don't believe this works in social media. Building huge lead lists is the old way of doing business.

When was the last time you saw a TV commercial, heard one on the radio, got a direct mail piece or saw it in a magazine or billboard and rushed to take action? We are inundated with ads in every aspect of our lives and so we've learned to glaze over and see around them. Whoa, but if somebody actually reaches out to you personally, it's HUGE. Let's say you complain about the service you got when you called customer relations about a faulty product. These days mention the brand name and it's quite possible you'll hear from a company representative in a flash. Why? Because companies that get social media understand the power of a negative comment. They also know that with just a tiny amount of personal attention to let you know they care about your woes, you're going to tell your network how responsive they are. There are countless examples of this on social media networks right now, and corporations as well as small businesses are trying to figure out how to make this work.

This whole idea of MLM seems to me to be so blatantly thoughtless that I refuse to friend anybody who appears to be doing it, much less buy a product from them.

There are many, many success stories of companies reaching out to individuals, instead of mass spamming them, until they buy their product. Be one of those success stories.

In order to connect effectively with the people in your own network and those of your network's network's network, you need to create relationships. You need to understand the needs, the pains and the joys of your community (your network is a community; did I forget to mention that?). You need to nurture these relationships with attention, caring and entertainment.

Yes, it sounds like work and it is, but the rewards are amazing and can be almost immediate.

I ran into someone at an event recently who had an issue with an automated teller at a local Bank of America branch. The bank manager couldn't help because he said the teller was maintained by an outside agency. Phone customer service couldn't help because she didn't have the account number on the checks she'd deposited.

She shared her issues on Twitter, mostly as a way of venting. @BofA_help heard her though, and within 24 hours she had a call from a VP in the customer service department who solved her problem.

Just two days later, @BofA_help helped me work through a billing snafoo that both the bank and customer service hadn't resolved, and returned nearly $500 in miss-assigned fees.

Since then I've referred several people to @BofA_help with good results.

What's the lesson?

Both my friend and I have become advocates for a brand we were ready to walk away from. One tweet and a positive result turned us around.

Dunbar Was Wrong

The question of how many connections you can effectively communicate with goes round and round in social media circles. The "Dunbar's Number" theory is frequently quoted as a measure of how many connections one person can really engage with at any one time. Usually by somebody who's having trouble managing what network they have now and can't imagine how they'll do it when their network gets bigger.

Dunbar's number is named after Robin Dunbar, a British anthropologist, who theorized that the average human brain could only effectively maintain a social relationship with approximately 150 people at one time. (Dunbar never actually set an exact number, but this is the one most frequently quoted.)

I wonder how these theories really relate to the communication tools we use today. I argue that social media enables us to reach out to many more people and make more relationships at a time. Although many of those relationships may not be as deep as family or close personal friends, they still enrich our lives and expand what we are able to experience.

Currently, I've got about 6,000 people at the first level of my various networks, and while I don't communicate regularly with all of them, I work hard to have some kind of connection and refresh the contact periodically in some way. My connections range widely in interest areas, as does my business, so each of these interest areas has its own sub-network as well. I may share some information or a connection within one of these subgroups, thus nurturing the relationship with the group and the people I've connected. Generally there will be some feedback, some give and take or conversation resulting from this, either on or offline. New introductions will be made and new conversations started.

I'm not supporting building humongous numbers of "friends" for the sake of the numbers. I will never support that kind of list building. What I am saying is: if you do have a large network, it's possible to connect effectively with a lot more people than 150.

Don't take my word for it, take Chuck Hester for example. Chuck is the author of 'LinkedIn Pay it Forward.' He's got over 9,000 people in just ONE of his networks, yet I know from experience he does actively engage a large number of his connections regularly. He created a local network called "LinkedIn Live" in Raleigh, North Carolina that attracts hundreds of people who connect face to face and talk about business and social media. These events are now held across the country.

Chuck regularly reaches out to his connections online, and he connects people who are looking for jobs or seeking services as a regular part of the maintenance of his network. Ask him a question and he probably has a resource for the answer.

Ari Herzog is another good example. On his blog, he talks about connecting with friends from social media connections face to face for the first time, and it feels like beers with long time co-workers. Why? Because he has already developed relationships with them online. They know about each other's jobs and family, challenges that need to be overcome and what their favorite topics are. Face-to-face conversations are just the next logical step.

Chuck and Ari are using social media to create real relationships with large networks and it works.

So what do you think? Are our meager brains limited in capacity to 150 connections? Or are they complex enough to a lot more? Do the tools we have now enable us to reach more people and still have real relationships? Then you'd better get started on that network.

How Do You Build an Effective Network?

Getting started building your network is actually simple. The hard part is figuring out exactly who you want in that network and where they "live" online. You see, you don't want to go out and join networks willy-nilly. It's a waste of your energy if your target market isn't there.

First you have to define the characteristics of the perfect customer, and then you do some research to find out where they are already having conversations.

Lastly, you break down all you have learned and decide which networks are the best use of your time and resources, create your profiles on these networks and stick your toe in the water to start the conversation.

Who Do You Want in Your Network?

Who is your perfect connection? What kinds of things do they like to talk about besides what you want to talk to them about? You need to collect a lot of demographics and get a picture of the personality profile, age group and interests of your potential friend base.

Do some surveys to find out what else they are interested in, but remember the demographics of surveys can be tainted by being only answered by people who answer surveys!

Do some research online as well. You want to gather as much as you can find out about who they are and what their interests are before going on to the next step.

In the example of David Armano's plea for help, David has a very carefully nurtured network full of people who know him at some level and like and trust him. The people in his network reached out to their own network and those people trusted the person they heard it from. If it had simply been a broadcast about a family in need and we didn't know anything about the blogger at all, would we have made a personal connection and donated?

Maybe, but you can bet there would have been fewer passionate blog posts and calls to rally the network to help, and the groundswell of aid would have been slower to occur.

6 Finding Your Network

Building an effective social media network seems pretty simple on the surface. You add everybody you know, right? Well, maybe, but it might be a good idea to bring in some new voices too. After all, you already know what your wife had for breakfast, right? Let's think a little more strategically than that.

What do you want to talk about? Sit down and think about what you talk about at work, at home, when you're speaking to clients and make a list of topics and keywords that are at the core of your day to day conversations. Include the keywords you use to talk about your business on your website, as well as a few of your off-hours pastimes. Make another list of business contacts or people you'd like to have time to talk to.

Now start searching. You're going to want to identify where people are talking about the topics you are interested in, what types of networks they are using and where the biggest concentration of interest is.

You can certainly do this with traditional search engines, but you're likely to have to wade through a lot of websites, press releases and static content to find the conversations. Instead, let's take a look at tools just for social media mentions. Some are free or low cost and others range from $100 to $1,000 a month.

SocialMention.com is usually my first go-to. It uses Yahoo's BOSS platform to search a variety of social media platforms. It searches social sites ranging from blogs and micro-blogs to forums, bookmarking sites, audios and videos. In real time. Almost everybody starts with a "vanity search," searching for their own name. Go ahead and do it. You might very well learn there are conversations going on out there about you that you didn't know about. If your name is Joe Brown, you may find there are a lot of Joe Browns.

You'll also see that Social Mention scores the results by "sentiment." They are running algorithms that detect the phrasing and use of particular words that tip the engine off to a positive or negative vibe to the discussion. Sometimes it's something like "I hate it when Joe Brown takes the team to the Laker's game and I can't go!" or "Joe Brown took the development team to a fabulous dinner to celebrate the product launch." As you can see, negative and positive sentiments are a subjective thing.

Search for a few of the keywords you came up with earlier and start making more lists. These are of where the conversations are, which are most relevant to you, and who is in the discussions. Some people find it useful to create a bookmark list of all the sites they find so they can quickly go back to them later.

Once you start to see a trend and specific keywords getting more discussion time than others, you might set up alerts on Social Mention to email you with new mentions of those keywords. I generally set up some in Google Alerts and the Twitter alert services too. (I'll get to those in a minute.) Create an email account just for alerts or set up filters so your email doesn't get swamped with alerts.

This basic searching may be enough for you to see what networks people are talking in that would be interesting to get in on. If there are conversations going on in forums or blogs, you can get in on the conversation right away and add your own thoughts to the mix.

It's still a good idea to dig a little deeper to get the big picture from several different listening tools, so I'll quickly go over some of them. It's up to you to decide which fits your needs best.

Mindmapping for Keywords

I'm going to use a winery as an example, but you can take the same concepts and apply them to any field.

How do you decide what to listen for if you want to get beyond your product, your brand and your own fine self?

You can use tools like Google's keyword tool, sites like Keyword-finder and several others, but I like to use mind-mapping tools for this.

First we sit down and do a little stream of consciousness keyword generation.

We come up with the top 5–6 keywords that relate to areas of interest we can talk about. They may or may not be loosely related to the company, the partners, or competitors or your clients.

I pulled this together based on what I know about the winery as a consumer; it is going to show you how I look at this business.

- The focus is especially on what potential connections are interested in.

- Trust me, your brand and your product are probably not first to mind.

- They may be looking for wine in a particular region or a place to picnic while they wine taste.

- They may be talking about food and wine pairing and looking for a good match.

- Maybe they're touring Santa Clara Valley on business and they want to find a place to taste, have a little picnic, and get some unusual entertainment to tell their friends about when they get home.

- Maybe they are musicians as well and they love to support other musicians.

Okay, so you've got a list of keywords.

Now you have to find out where people are talking about these things.

Are they on Wine blogs? Forums about musicians, soccer or cricket? Facebook, Twitter or communities like Ning groups?

To find out you need to do some searches and set up some alerts to let you know where a topic is being discussed.

Real-time Search

Social media moves very quickly, and while traditional search and alerts are fine for finding existing conversations, sometimes you want to get up to the minute results.

Lazyfeed searches RSS feeds from blogs and Twitter to video and image feeds. Do real-time searches on pretty much any topic, and if the results are intriguing, save the search for later. Put in a few keywords or phrases and you'll quickly see which float to the top as the most often discussed. Save the searches you like for later and they'll be updated when you come back to review again.

Lazyfeed will also help you find relative topics based on your interests on your social networks. Look into the topics tab where you can connect your Twitter, Flickr, Delicious accounts or blogs. Lazyfeed searches these sites for tags in those accounts and streams them live into your topics feed.

Monitter and Yahoo! Sideline are real-time search engines for Twitter. Enter keywords, names, and corporate brands and see a real time list of Tweets on those topics. These are incredibly useful ways to track what's going on at a conference, breaking news events or current discussions about your keywords.

Twendz and Trendrr are two more real time Twitter engines that show which topics are trending with a lot of discussion about them. Although these tend to be celebrity gossip, on occasion they can also be useful for breaking news.

Tweetbeep allows you to save multiple alerts for a keyword, phrase or domain name on Twitter and can be filtered by distance from a location, particular usernames and whether or not a URL is in the post. These alerts can be emailed to you on a scheduled or real-time basis and are very useful in alerting you to a new discussion or reference.

There are also real time monitoring tools that let you quickly search for breaking events, and you can also do a real time search to see if someone is talking about you while they are standing in line. Several cases have been reported of Southwest Air and Jet Blu where someone was standing in line, late for their gate at the airport and com-plaining on Twitter. Someone who was listening for the airline on Twitter caught it in real time, contacted the ticket counter and resolved the situation on the spot.

Don't think for a second that THAT story didn't get shared and re-shared as a customer service success. It's a win win for everybody, right?

People are beginning to actually expect this kind of service, and if you don't provide it they're going to look for someone who does.

Before you groan and tell me you don't get Twitter and don't want to use it, let me say that you don't have to Tweet to take advantage of Twitter. Whether you tweet or not, you can't afford not to listen to it.

Twitter can give you real time issues as in the case just discussed; it's very keyword focused and a huge source for inbound links and links to information you may have missed if you weren't looking for them.

Tweeting is not for everybody, but at least include it in your listening campaign.

Deeper Search and Metrics Tools

The Search Monitor watches paid searches, blogs, news, and websites and offers a more complex search, all wrapped up in a spiffy interface, for those reports you need to write. Site monitor keeps an eye on your paid search keywords as well as those of your competitors, and creates a number of reports for affiliate compliance, brand buzz, ad copy, trademark use, and market share and delivers them in a clean interface to view all at once or in email alerts to keep you on top of things.

BuzzLogic tracks conversations in social media and helps identify the key influencers talking about your brand or your product space. Their Insights reporting tools give you a dashboard full of information about who's saying what and where these conversations are taking place. Create a Watch list of your favorite influencers, view social maps of who is participating in the discussion and set up profiles for bloggers you want to track. BuzzLogic also offers ad targeting programs to deliver your ads to the conversations you want to be in on.

Radian6 is full on social media metrics dashboard complete with the ability to manage workflow by assigning tasks like responding to a particular post to other team members, adding notes for the engagement you took, and classifying any sentiment related to the post.

You can create some very deep search functions and get alerts as well as their "river of news" which shows you all of the conversations around your chosen search topics in an organized stream.

The service is chock full of ways to look at metrics, from using Backtype.com's comment indexing engine to integrating with your Compete.com website traffic statistics.

You can segment your analytics in a number of ways and really squeeze a lot of valuable data out of the interactions. Oh, and it turns out beautiful reports too. Just what the CXOs need for the board meeting!

That said, some of the big metrics tools may be an over-kill for small businesses. If you don't get a ton of results in your searches and a lot of traffic to the site, those metrics are hard to divine meaning from, and it's not cheap to get into these solutions.

Trackur keeps track of the keywords you're most interested in, whether they are on blogs, websites, videos or even as images, so you can keep track of how your logo is being used online.

The filters allow you to quickly hone results down to just what you want to see.

Alerts can be delivered by RSS feed or email and your searches can be exported as a CSV for saving, sorting or creating reports.

You can also bookmark results to go back to at a later date. Trackur is an inexpensive alternative, but they really can keep up with the big boys. If you're on a budget, this is an excellent resource.

Techrigy's SM2

Very much like Radian6 and Trackur, SM2 (except that SM2 was designed specifically for PR and marketing professionals) delivers insights into site monitoring with sentiment analysis and custom reporting.

They also offer a feature they call "Discussion Clustering" which gives you a graphical analysis of conversations going on so you can see the scope and crossover between authors and discussions.

7 Choosing the Right Venues

So you've listened carefully and you've got a long list of people you want to connect with. You've sorted them out and discovered they are mostly on 2–3 different networks and many are on both. Now what do you do?

Even if you find these deep conversations about your niche on 3, 6 or even 10 different networks, don't feel you have to engage on all of them at once. Take your time. Figure out which network will work best for your personal skill set, the time available and the content you already have before you start.

Not everybody needs Twitter, a Facebook page or their own set of forums. Sure there are lots of people who will tell you their favorite network tool is essential to your social media campaign, but that's not necessarily so. Maybe it's just that it's essential to **their** social media style.

Once you've done your listening and figured out where your target market is having conversations, see which of these sites feels comfortable to you. Do you find the interface easy to understand? Do you like the way people talk to each other and share information or does it seem too clubby, too noisy or too technical? Give this some time to settle in. If you don't know how to use the site, you can deal with that, but if you don't like the flavor of the conversation or the way users interact, it might not be the network for you.

Another thing to think about is who is already talking in your industry on this particular site. Let's say you search the Ning groups for one that deals with your particular area of interest and find nothing. You can look at this in two ways: People who use Ning aren't interested in your widget, or it's an opportunity to start a community on Ning and everybody else who searches for that topic will find only you waiting to talk to them. You have to decide if you want to jump in and take that risk, or pass and go on to one of the other networks you discovered in your listening phase.

If you find a network or forum where people are asking questions in your industry and nobody's answering, it may be a golden opportunity to engage.

Sometimes you find a brand-new social media platform and there isn't anybody in your space as yet in your space. Take a good look before you commit resources to this new platform; if it seems stable and they've got an interface and "voice" that appeals to you, this may be an opportunity to be the leader in your space on this particular network.

Honestly, I like to give them a little time first and see if they get a lot of people signing up (adoption rate) before I commit time and resources to starting a new presence on an untested platform. Do some comparisons with other networks that seem similar and see if you get a good feeling about them. Trust your gut or ask around on other networks before you jump.

If you really think you've found the next new bright star, go ahead and investigate. Set up a profile and see how it feels to you and if the people who join the network seem like a good fit. Just remember to distribute your efforts between the established networks and the new ones.

What Have You Got to Work With?

When you're figuring out how you want to use social media sites, you need to be honest about your time and resources. Can you commit to a schedule? How much time can you devote? Do you already have content available that you can re-purpose for your social media efforts? (See the section on content for ideas.) Is your team up to the challenge of spreading the word throughout their own networks?

Are You Sure You Want to Do This?

This is work. You have to spend time nurturing your network and you can't be insincere about it. You have to care enough about your network to let them know you'll help them if they need it, and they will return the favor. You have to take the time to really engage, develop relationships and follow up leads. You have to really want to be part of the relationship. If they even sniff insincerity or disguised sales techniques, you're toast. If they discover you hired a consultant to pretend they are you because you're too busy, they may very well feel betrayed. If you can't make time to engage, find somebody in your company who does. If it's not something the company is ready to commit to, it's better to put it off than do it badly.

As much as social media is the heart and soul of the way I do business, it just might not be right for the way you run YOUR business.

Traditional marketing methods are all about getting the product in front of as many eyeballs as possible. Preferably with a catchy enough slogan or design to differentiate yourself from the herd. Failing that, some marketers turn to volume. If you can reach millions of people every day on Twitter or Facebook for FREE, why not take advantage of that opportunity to get eyeball share by setting up scheduled messaging to hit people at varying times of day, see which time slot gets the most clicks and then bombard that time slot with special offers until you get some sales? Why not get as many followers, friends and connections as possible, so you can use those numbers in your marketing reports? Isn't it all about metrics?

Doing so makes it crystal clear that you don't get social media, and you may actually be doing your brand more damage than you think. Go ahead, try it if you must, and watch people simply un-friend, un-follow and turn their backs on you. You can be shut out of the herd in a blink of an eye if you don't contribute something real to the community. Oh, and don't think they won't be talking about you after you go, just not the way you might have hoped. Don't think it will be easy to win them back either.

Social media is just that. It's social. It's about relationships between individuals, not companies.

Everybody talks about how Comcast turned their customer service reputation around by setting up the Comcast Cares account on Twitter. But it wasn't Comcast that did it. It was Frank Eliason, setting out on his own to solve a problem. He wasn't trying to make sales. He was trying to solve a problem, and it was his personal responses on a one-on-one level that made it work. It did work. It worked brilliantly. Because of Frank's personal attention and now his team's, there are countless examples of companies and individuals mimicking Frank's efforts. Some successful and some not.

If you're not willing to actually take the time to talk to your potential customers, social media "marketing" isn't for you. In fact, strike the phrase Social Media Marketing from your vocabulary. As many people as there are right now willing to make a fast buck by telling you that the answer to your prayers is Social Media Marketing, I'm here to call bullsh*t on that one right now. It's not marketing. It's communicating. It's creating friendships and relationships and being a valuable part of the society you decide to take part in. It's listening to your customers and what they say to each other and then responding or acting on what you've learned to deepen their trust in you. It may even extend to giving them a place to complain about you, so you can listen and make your product better.

When you give more to the community than you expect in return, you can establish a place of respect. From that place, people will look to your product because they like, trust and respect you and they know that if there's a problem with the product, you'll be there to stand behind your brand. It's kind of like going back to the small town days when the local merchant knew the names and desires of every customer. He knew that if he sold a bad product, the community would spread the word and he'd be out of business, but if he reached out in good faith to give his customers the best he possibly could, they would return with faith and loyalty. If you're not willing to make that commitment for your customers, social media is not for you.

Chapter 7: Choosing the Right Venues

8 Set Some Rules (or at least Guidelines)

I'm a big fan of a corporate policy for social media for any business, no matter how small. Unless there's only one person who will be handling your social media efforts, you need to set some guidelines in place. Now, by this I don't mean you have to write a huge document that strangles any hint of spontaneity from your team. Quite the opposite. A corporate policy lets them know what they need to know to communicate the company message effectively, and what they should and should not do.

People Are More Comfortable Knowing the Rules

I've encountered staff on many occasions who were simply terrified of social media. Where to start? What to say? How to use the tools and would they get into trouble? A little guidance and training and they were just fine. Use your social media engagement policy as a way to show them the ropes and give them models to follow.

Three Good Reasons for a Social Media Corporate Policy

1. Set branding standards for communication

Clearly you can't have people making up their own logos and color schemes for your company. If your marketing department has a style guide, put the best bits in your corporate policy document. It saves everybody a lot of headaches if they can create a profile with a company-approved logo and a color scheme that reflects the company without any guessing. Make the resources they need available and they'll be more likely to dive in and you won't have to assign a hall monitor.

2. Educate your team

What terms do you use to describe your product? Are there any particular industry or work-related terms you need to have associated with the product? Are there terms you NEVER want used with your product? Here's where you educate the team. Somebody from production may have no idea of the carefully worded press release you just sent out, in which you said the margin for error in your product was 0.006 %, but he may know the last test results he saw were 0.02%. Make sure everybody has the facts so they can put your best foot forward.

3. Set expectations for behavior

Again, if people know the rules and what is expected from them, they are less likely to make mistakes. State clearly what standards of performance you expect. A little personal responsibility and some common sense go a long way. This also sets the corporate naysayers a bit more at ease.

I'm not saying you should get all draconian with your team in what they can and cannot say. This is very hard to understand for many larger corporations where the legal department approves every press release and the PR department approves every statement on the website before it can go live. Social media doesn't work like this. If your statements appear to be canned or professionally produced, they are bound to fall flat. Let the team know the facts when a new product comes out or when you reach a noteworthy milestone. Then let them put it into their own words.

What goes into a typical corporate social media policy doc?

Rather than blather on, here are some examples to learn from. Scan for ideas and adapt to fit your own needs.

Intel did a fabulous job with their social media guidelines. It's obvious what they expect, and the whole thing is in clear, easy-to-understand language. They actually offer a training course called the Digital IQ training conducted by their "Social Media Center of Excellence."

Here's an excerpt from their website:

If you participate in social media, please follow these guiding principles:

- Stick to your area of expertise and provide unique, individual perspectives on what's going on at Intel and in the world.

- Post meaningful, respectful comments—in other words, no spam and no remarks that are off-topic or offensive.

- Always pause and think before posting. That said, reply to comments in a timely manner, when a response is appropriate.

- Respect proprietary information and content, and confidentiality.

- When disagreeing with others' opinions, keep it appropriate and polite.

- Know and follow the Intel Code of Conduct and the Intel Privacy Policy.

Simple, clean and easy to grasp, isn't it?

Sample Corporate Policies

For responding to a blog comment, the U.S. Air Force social media policy is complete with flow charts that are as detailed as one might expect from the government. They have specific guidelines for their "BlueTube" video site, Wikipedia and several other networks.

Minneapolis' Walker Art Center's blogging guidelines clearly state the goals of the Walker's blogs, with advice on finding images and copyright issues, and refers to the Electronic Frontier Foundation's legal guide for bloggers. They don't over-control; they support, encourage and enable their staff to make good choices and speak freely.

The BBC has a hands-off approach to personal blogs as long as the writer does not identify themselves with the BBC on their personal blog. Staff is allowed to talk about programs, etc., but is required to include a disclaimer for personal editorial comments on blogs.

On other networks, the BBC staff is encouraged to be sensitive and professional:

We should be sensitive to the expectations of existing users of the specific site. If we add a BBC presence, we are joining their site rather than the opposite. Users are likely to feel that they already have a significant stake in it. When adding an informal BBC presence, we should "go with the grain" and be sensitive to user customs and conventions to avoid giving the impression that the BBC is imposing itself on them and their space.

For example, we should respect the fact that users on site X are not our users; they are not bound by the same Terms of Use and House Rules as we apply on bbc.co.uk. Attempts to enforce our standard community rules on third party sites may lead to resentment, criticism and in some cases outright hostility to the BBC's presence.

This is not to say that behaviour likely to cause extreme offence, for example racist insults, should be tolerated by the BBC on a BBC branded space on a social networking site. It should not.

Neither should behaviour which is clearly likely to put a child or teenager at substantial risk of significant harm. But where we do decide to intervene, we will normally need to do so with a light touch, sensitive to different expectations and a different context from bbc.co.uk.

Style Guides

Style guides have been around for ages in the advertising and design world. Many corporations have style guides that designate how everything—from the logo to fonts and color—is to be used in relationship to the company, and I can tell you that working with such a style guide can save a lot of headaches, for both the management and the vendor or employee who has to implement it.

A lot of this is done for branding purposes and is very serious stuff. For example, can the logo be black and white? Can it be cut up and stacked if it doesn't fit in the available area? What are the colors associated with the corporate brand? What are the preferred fonts used in communication? If you don't already have one, I suggest you give it a little thought. It doesn't have to be heavy handed, but it's a lot easier to supply your bloggers and social media advocates with the material they need to set up pages and profiles without having to police them to make sure they get it right.

Along with the style guide, it's a good idea to post copies of often-used images, logos and fonts somewhere on an intranet or download site, so everybody has access to the style guide and the materials they need to comply with.

Pick Your Team

Something that's all too common when a company first gets into social media is to bring all the youngest people in the company together and make them the social media team. After all, they're young so they must understand this stuff, right?

Well, maybe so and maybe not; just because they have a MySpace page doesn't mean they understand social media concepts. More importantly, do they understand how to create relationships for your company? Will they know the answers to questions that come up about your services, or will they need to have a resource on the team to go to with these questions? Are these the people you want to trust with your reputation?

A little training can go a long way, either for these young team members or your more experienced team who may just need a coaching session or two to get their sea legs and get to work.

What you really want to look for are the people who are already natural relationship builders and have a good knowledge of the company offerings and the value you offer to potential clients. Look for your in-house evangelists and empower them. Once you've got them set up with the tools they need, step back and let them run with it. Even if you don't entirely agree with the direction they are going, give them a little space to grow before you rein them in. They may go places you never thought you could.

Insource or Outsource?

This is a big question. Some companies simply aren't staffed to allow for a full or even part-time social media person. So is it okay to out-source? If it's a decision to engage or not even try because you don't have the time or ability to participate, then you need to take a really close look at what's going on in your business space. What are your competitors doing and how does that affect your decision? What's your marketing budget and could the savings of using social media offset hiring someone to help you with this?

Hired Guns

Bringing in a marketer with an established social media presence can be a good idea to help you make informed decisions. Bringing in somebody who's been in the trenches and knows how the networks work can help you decide which avenues are the best opportunities and to brainstorm ideas to get off the ground effectively. Then you're in a better position to decide who will do the work and how much you want to expend financially and of company time.

Finding a consultant is a difficult task. There are loads of consultants who will tell you they know all that there is to social networking, but with a little searching you find they've got a relatively small social media presence or even none at all. There are also social media certification courses they can take that will supposedly teach them all they need to know. Don't believe it even for a second.

While it's possible that someone could be a certified business coach who uses social media, I firmly believe there are no "experts" in social media and that certification is absolutely meaningless. By the time the courses go through the process of development and presentation and the first student graduates, there are a dozen new networks popping up or the configuration of the existing ones will have changed. In order to get a clear picture of what's out there, you need somebody who lives and breathes this stuff.

Fortunately there are several people who do live and breathe social media, and because they do, they're not really that hard to find. I'm going back to those listening tools again. Spend some time looking at who is having the conversations in your area of interest. Spend a little more time Googling the names of the people you are considering hiring to help you with your campaign.

Set up a phone call to chat and see what they say about networks. If they say "You HAVE to have a ___ account," find out why they think that. No social media person should tell you where you need to participate until they know a little about your business, your needs and resources. If they try to sell you their favorites, it may be all they know. Ask a lot of questions and see how you feel.

Finally, ask for references and call them. Find out what they liked and didn't like. How did they measure success and did they feel they learned something? Were they satisfied they were dealing with a professional who really cared about their business or did they feel like the consultant was learning it all on the fly?

To be fair here, there are way too many networks for any of us to know all of them, how they work and what the best fit is right away. A good consultant will be willing to tell you that and then go do their homework.

Once you've settled on someone to pull together your strategy, you can work with them to find the networks and connections you need, identify existing material that can be optimized into blog posts, white papers, video clips (instead of long movies) etc. Hopefully you'll work together to come up with a plan to bring it all together in a reasonable timeline that works for you. Ask them if they or their team can coach you through how to use the various apps and networks and give you strategies to engage effectively.

It's not at all unusual for someone new to social media to need some coaching in the beginning. There are different cultures between the various networks, and your consultant (better yet, coach!) should know the difference between the cultures of Facebook and LinkedIn for example, and they should be able to explain it to you and help you tweak your content to suit whom you are talking to.

Ghostwriters

This is a hugely controversial topic. Ghostwriters are people who write for you under your name and ghost writing goes way back in the history of writing. It's not new that people who "don't have time" or "can't write" hire someone to do their writing for them. Some ghostwriters have been hugely successful. So much so that when they quit writing for the person they were ghosting for, that person had to "retire" or lose their readership.

I'm not 100% against ghost writing. There are times it's okay to bring someone in to assist, but I'm adamant that it's not okay for all of your social media presence to be the work of someone else! If your customer builds a relationship with a ghost blogger, where does that relationship end? What about when that customer picks up the phone to talk to you and it's not "you"? What happens when that person says something that inadvertently damages your reputation? What happens when they're sick or quit and you have to replace them with another "you"?

Relationships are about trust, so if you're going to bring in a writer to help you, make it clear they work for you. They can use the company name, you can give them a title like "community outreach specialist" or "online advocate," but don't say it's you, because when people discover this, they'll burn you at the virtual stake.

Take Guy Kawasaki, for example. Back in the early days of Twitter, he really did post on his own a lot, and his posts were engaging and sometimes just fun tidbits of odd stuff he found. After a while though, it just got to be too much, so Guy hired some people to help find interesting information. Then he started Alltop.com and again he had a team helping him find the blogs that get listed there.

Now Guy's a smart guy and when people finally asked him if it was really all him posting all this stuff he fessed right up. In fact, he told everybody who the ghosters were and made it clear they were an important part of his team. There was a dust-up at first of course, but eventually people either quit following him on Twitter or just accepted it.

Here's my take on that. The posts Guy was sending out were interesting and they still are. Do I have a relationship with him? Nope, I actually filter his Twitter stream into a column in Seesmic called fun stuff and read it when I need a lift. Thanks, Guy.

By the way, Guy's book, 'Reality Check,' is another one on my must-read list. He doesn't pull his punches and he speaks in plain English, with a hefty dash of humor.

"Focus on the customer. Here's what most people find surprising: The best way to drive your competition crazy is not to do anything to it. Rather, the best way is for you to succeed, because your success, more than any action, will drive your competition crazy." – Guy Kawasaki – 'Reality Check'

Bottom line, is ghosting okay? I think it's okay as long as the ghost is intended to collect and disseminate information, but if you want them to engage and create relationships, you have to tell people whom they are engaging with. If it's not you and it's one of the engineers or a person in marketing, let them be themselves. Nobody said the CEO has to blog, so if it's not comfortable for you, have somebody else do it.

What's the lesson?

The rules for hiring ghostwriters are very similar to the ones for hired guns. Make sure they can represent you and they know the format you're asking them to work with. Having a personal MySpace page is very different from blogging for a corporation. Get work samples and call references. Oh, and ask who else they're ghosting for. You don't want to use the same writer as your competition!

Working with Your Content

Unlike some other media sources, social media likes information in small bites. It's one of the attractions to micro-blogs like Twitter. Deliver information succinctly and give me a link to follow if I want more information. Give me 5–1 minute videos to download instead of a 1–5 minute video. This is good news for you.

Take some of the longer content you already have like white papers and similar information and split it up for delivery in multiple forms. Maybe some gets Tweeted with a link to download a white paper. Break it up and convert it to blog posts. Pull the best points out and share with an image on micro-blogs like Posterous, Tumblr etc.

A Word About SEO

Search Engine Optimization (SEO) is a huge topic and I'm not going to go in depth here, but let me just say that social media will blow you away with its capacity to improve organic search results. (Organic search results are listings that are not paid to be displayed.)

I've done some unscientific tests and found Twitter posts to show up in a Google Search within 15 minutes, and blog posts and comments are almost as fast. Forums tend to take a little more time to show up and there are a lot of variables with other social networks as to how quickly they are indexed by the search engines, etc. Rather than go deeply into SEO and social media now (that's for the next book), I'll give you a quick overview. I'm going to go into detail about the various tools later, so if you don't understand how a particular piece of the puzzle works, skip ahead to read it or skim over this now to come back to later.

For the sake of argument, let's say one of your social media goals is to increase your own visibility and that of your business through social media.

You want to be seen as a thought leader and a resource for people interested in your field of expertise.

You want to drive traffic to your blog and your website through various social networking tools.

You've got a lot of written material already, some videos, some white papers, maybe even some webinars, and you're ready to write more.

You've already scoped out the networks you're interested in and you want to blog on, have an existing Twitter presence, a LinkedIn profile and participate on various forums and groups.

For this case, you can create a network of links that feed each other traffic and gently funnel that traffic towards your blog and your website. You set up your website and your blog as the center of your own network of sites.

You're going to write up a few blog posts with information that will be valuable to your network. These don't have to be long. In fact, from an SEO standpoint, they are more valuable if they're short, to the point and rich with information and keywords. You've got a great product demo so you upload that to YouTube. You've got pictures of the team and the new product, and you upload those to Flickr.

Your blog is the central point of presence in this universe.

When you make a blog post, you let your Twitter network know by posting a link to the blog post on Twitter. Use the title of the post and some carefully chosen phrasing to make it interesting and keyword appropriate. (Meaning the words you use need to actually be an important part of the post!)

Depending on the blog platform you're using, you will either manually or automatically ping Technorati to let it know you've written something new. You should also have tools like pingomatic set up to automatically update the search engines and blog catalog services that you've posted something new.

Your Twitter and blog RSS feeds should be set up to automatically go to FriendFeed and your LinkedIn profile.

Post a complementary post on Posterous with additional useful information and use Posterous's feeds to auto post it to Twitter, LinkedIn, Delicious, Reddit, tumblr and StumbleUpon.

Get accounts at MyBlogLog and Blog Catalog and add your RSS feed to help spread the word about your new post.

Post the videos you will use in your blog on YouTube, Vimeo, Seesmic or other video posting venues and then pick one to import into your blog.

Post the pictures to Flickr and tag the people in them so they will know the images are posted and can share them and your posts with their networks.

Hopefully other blogs will find your post interesting and link to it with their own comments. They may also link to your Flickr images or the videos.

Now go out looking for other blogs in the same space and add your voice in the comments section. If you're signed up with Backtype or Disqus, any comments you make will be tracked, and links to your comments and the blog they are on will show up on Backtype's site.

Clip interesting posts and share them in Amplify or Twitter or FriendFeed. You don't want to share exactly the same thing to all your networks. You want to add something a little different so you are adding value for your followers. You're trying to show you are a valuable resource in their networks with good links to appropriate on-topic information they want to have. Vary which of your sites you link to, so posts are exposed to different parts of your networks.

If someone links to your post from their blog or Twitter, go there and say thank you. Add value to the discussion there if you can, and remember that blogger. Maybe you can find something in common and write on a similar topic to keep the conversation rolling. As you develop more of these relationships, it will be come easier and easier to find something to blog about because your conversations will be deeper and richer and better for everyone involved.

Link to all of these different posts and comments in social bookmarking sites like Delicious, Reddit, and StumbleUpon and encourage your co-workers and network to do the same if they find it interesting.

Use Amplify to clip an excerpt of a site or blog you like and post it for discussion on the Amplify site. You can also clip your own posts here occasionally, but it's bad form to only clip your own posts!

Use Tumblr to post images and short posts that relate to your area of interest and link them back to your site. These should have different content than the blog, but should generally be about the same focused topics. Do the same thing on Posterous.

Wow! Seems like a load of work, doesn't it? Well, it's not really. If you paid attention, you'll see that once the accounts are set up, a lot of this is done automatically through RSS feeds and auto posts, leaving you to reply and respond, carry on conversations on other blogs, Twitter and groups on LinkedIn where you can be building relationships as well as traffic.

The majority of the network will buzz along quite happily on its own, and as people discover your bookmarks and posts, they'll subscribe to your feeds and start to talk with you, making your conversations richer and the search engines happier as they bounce from link to link all enhanced with keyword-rich content and conversations.

This will pay off fairly quickly in focused traffic to your blog and a higher visibility for you on your chosen topic in the search engines. Expect to see results in 3–6 months with a definite impact on traffic, and—more importantly—user interaction.

Again, let me remind you, this is just one scenario. There is no magic bullet, and there are thousands of possible variations. You need to look at the resources and time you have available and then investigate the networks to see which will work for you.

Stacey Kannenberg, aka the "Ready To Learn Mom," is an excellent example of building personal brand through social media.

Stacy founded Cedar Valley Publishing: Mom Central Consulting; Stacey Kannenberg Unlimited; and Mother Talk and she has leveraged her understanding of relationship development and social media to build a multi-million dollar presence using social media and spending very little money on traditional marketing. Her books have been reviewed by hundreds of bloggers and sold over 60,000 copies distributed internationally in several languages.

Stacey works very hard to keep her "Google footprint" established, so that both, she and her companies are easy to find and she has used social media heavily to keep visible, build her brand and keep her finger on the pulse of what women are doing online.

She uses member sites as one of the principal ways to grow her networks, belonging to 40 plus sites: The Mom Entrepreneur Group, Moms in Business, Woman Owned Businesses, Savor the Success, National Association of Woman Business Owners (NAWBO), Make Mine A Million, Work At Home Mom (WAHM), Home Based Working Mom (HBWM), The Joy of Connecting, Mom Inventors, Moms Town, Twitter Moms, Hybrid Moms, Moms-for-Profit, Blog-Her, as well as social networking sites on Ning, Twitter, Facebook and LinkedIn, JacketFlap, and ShoutLife to name a few!

Some of these profiles have 1000 to 25,000 views, and when you multiple that by 40, you have some serious exposure! Take that.

She's a very active blogger and Twitter user, which helps her build traffic directly to her sites, let people know of media appearances, and get the word out about her passion, getting ready to learn.

What's the lesson?

Creating your own network of information and then sharing and cross-sharing them with different sites can increase the visibility of your brand, making it a whole lot easier to get your message heard.

So let's get a little more specific about individual points in your network.

9 Twitter

Twitter is one of my favorite networks, but it certainly didn't start that way. At first, I just didn't get it at all. I followed a few friends and searched the main Twitter stream for interesting things to read, but mostly it was either about their cat, what they had for lunch, what they were going to have for their lunch or a link to the latest YouTube video of somebody doing something stupid. How in the world was this going to be useful for my business?

I did a few Google searches to see what other people were saying, and through those searches found some interesting bloggers, started following them and that's when it got interesting. You see, they were having conversations, but until I followed a few of them at one time, I didn't see the thread of the conversation at all and it was all lost in the rest of the noise.

After I learned the ropes a little, I started to talk to people too and hey, they talked back! I started paying attention to people talking about things I was interested in and following people who had worthwhile things to say. It didn't take long to hone in on the leaders in the online marketing and PR business, the web designers, and of course, the journalists.

As time passed, I found that new people were following me too and my network started to take on a life of its own. People just dive into conversations on Twitter, and that's perfectly okay. Think of it as a huge networking event with tight little clusters of people standing around, talking about different topics. Perhaps at a networking event you might feel you were intruding, but on Twitter, you can listen in and add your own 2 cents if it's useful and they'll be happy to have your input.

The key here is to be useful—don't dive in, drop your business cards and move on to the next group. That's rude at networking events and just plain silly on Twitter. If you don't have anything useful to say, just listen! We'll get to strategies to meet people on Twitter in a minute or two.

So what's the lesson in my early Twitter experiences?

1. Twitter is deadly boring until you find the right people to talk to, and you may have to do some homework to do that.
2. People do want to talk to you as long as you're saying something useful.

Before I get to how to find people to talk to on Twitter, let's talk about some very basic things you have to do first. The most important thing you can do before you start following people is to get your Twitter landing page done. Bio, picture, links to important info and a color scheme, all help tell your story. When somebody is deciding to follow you or not, they're going to come to this page to see who you are. If it's a default background and goggle-eyed icon, they're not going to be impressed.

Choose your username.

This may seem unimportant, but on Twitter it's your brand. The good news is it's possible to change it, but why start a network brand and change the name people are used to? Give a little thought to whom you are representing and how you want to be perceived.

Should you use your business name, your nickname, your cat's name or your own?

Well, you really do have to answer that one, but if you are representing your company, they may already have some guidelines. Unless you are representing the whole company's presence on Twitter yourself, it might not be such a hot idea to use the company brand name. However, if you're the marketing person responsible for getting the word out, then you might want to follow the lead of Coca Cola. Their bio clearly states, "A consolidation of the official tweets of The Coca-Cola Company," so even though their Tweets are relatively personal, we know it's more than one person. In fact the team members use their initials to identify themselves. "Adam here from Coke. I do have an XBOX 360 at home. Playing a LOT of Fight Night during the past two weeks! ^AB" identifies that Adam B is tweeting this particular post.

Many companies prefer their staff to use their own names and identify they are with the company when tweeting corporate information. I like this better because I can develop a relationship with one of the team members instead of having to sift through all the Tweets in their "Tweet Stream" to find the person I want to connect with. Zappos, Best Buy, Coke, all have multiple members tweeting and they have individual personalities and accounts, even though they represent the company.

Once you figure this out, log in and go to the settings page.

Profile image

The thumbnail icon that is your avatar is the other way people are going to decide if you're interesting or not. If they see your shining face along with influential discussions in their area of interest, they're going to remember you and want to talk to you. Take a quick look through Twitter to see the incredible variety here. You can use the company logo, but it's really not as interesting as you are. Twitter is a place of one-on-one conversations. People want to know who you are. Use a casual shot with some personality.

It's been interesting to go to meet-ups or even trade shows and have people flag me down because they recognize me from my picture on a network, without ever having met in person. People identify you with your avatar, like it or not.

Background image and colors

These may reflect the brand of your company or the fact you have a passion for images from the Hubble telescope. Either is fine. You have some real estate to work with on the left-hand side of the page. Many people put additional information here. It's not clickable, but you can use it to let them know more about you, perhaps something more than that which is in your short bio.

There are services to help set up a good Twitter background, or you can make your own with a simple large image.

How to Tweet

I'm stunned that even after all this time Twitter doesn't send out a welcome message with basic instructions on how to use their service. It would be really simple, but I guess they think it's intuitive. It's not.

How to post on the Twitter website

Log in with your username and password. See that box that says "What are you doing?" That's where you'll make your posts. At first, if you're not following anybody, that's pretty much all you're going to see. I'll give you more on how to find people to follow now, but to not get too off track, let's say you have 10 people's email addresses and you want to follow them.

Click the link for "find people" at the top of the page. Here you can search for a company name, a person's name, or a username. You can also search your other networks for names to add here. Twitter search will look through the database for names that are close and bring up a list. Click the names to go to their page and learn more, or click the follow button to follow them. They will get a message letting them know you've started following them and they will likely follow you back or at least look at your profile to learn more.

Once you've followed someone, you'll start seeing their Tweets in your Twitter stream (on your Twitter home page). These are only the tweets of the people you follow. Until they follow you back, they probably won't see yours at all. Don't follow a bazillion people right off the bat. If you haven't said anything interesting yet, why would they want to follow you? Choose your Twitter friends carefully for the value they add to you and your network. Take your time. You're looking to build relationships, not notches in your cyber bedpost.

Start Tweeting

To send a message to your network in general, just put your thoughts in the text entry box and hit update. Really, it's that simple. If you want to send a link though, I recommend you use a URL shortening tool like tinyURL, Bit.ly, Ow.ly or Su.pr (Google them) to make the URL short and not take up too many of your precious 140 characters.

If you want to send a message to someone or reply to something they said, you put an @ sign in front of their username, and a space followed by your message.

"@Username My message is really simple. Here's a link: http://bit.ly/O9Zil."

This message goes out to everyone and ends up in the main Twitter stream as well as in the "mentions" window of the person you sent it to.

If you want to send a semi-private message (there is no privacy on the Internets) then you put a d a space, their username and the message. These are called Direct Messages or DM's for short.

"D username How are you? Heard you weren't feeling so hot."

It is a very good idea to never send a DM you want to be absolutely private. People inadvertently mis-type this all the time and send those messages out to the world. Or the person you are sending it to may, by mistake, reply instead of direct messaging you back.

Re-tweets are another way to send a message and they are really important. A re-tweet is when you find a link of comment so valuable, you want to share it with your own network of followers. Copy the entire message, including the username, and paste it in the message window. At the very beginning of the message, put RT a space, the @sign and the user it came from.

"RT: @username then quote exactly what they said here. Do not edit unless you have to fit it in."

When you write a Tweet, make sure there is room for it to get re-tweeted. That means leave at least 20–40 characters at the end, so when someone re-tweets it to their network, they don't have to shorten your Tweet.

Say please and thank you. If you want a post re-tweeted, it's more likely to happen if you say "Please RT." Of course, this means your post has to be that much shorter. Always thank people for re-tweeting or mentioning you. It doesn't have to be a reply, it can be a direct message or even an email or a phone call. Let them know you appreciate their time and sharing your Tweet with their network.

Don't steal somebody else's Tweet without giving them credit. Either say RT @jfouts and then quote the tweet verbatim (don't edit somebody else's Tweet unless you have to make it short enough) or give the title and then (via @jfouts) as a credit. The only exception to this is if the Tweet has been re-tweeted several times, and then you can credit the original tweeter.

Hashtags were born to help Twitter users track specific conversations. It's quite common these days for a conference to post the hashtag for the event prominently, so everybody can "tag" their comments to the conference. Actually it's pretty cool to do a search for a conference and see a virtual stream of comments following presentation after presentation and it can be a great way to feel like you're right there. To find out what Hashtags are currently being used, go to Hashtags.org and do a search. Click the links that come up with a tag and you'll see all the conversations that included that tag.

To use a hashtag is really simple. Say you went to the Online Community Conference 2009.

The tag includes the # sign and the tag itself, no spaces, then your message.

"#OCU09 was amazing again this year. I always learn so much and meet amazing people. Thank you Forum One!"

Not only does this Tweet show up in hashtags on Twitter, but the search engines pick up hashtags too.

That's it. Now that post will be forever linked with the event on Twitter—ready to be helpful to someone deciding if they are going to go to the next conference or not!

Okay, that covers the basics. I advise people to find about 10–20 people they are interested in first, and then just listen and participate on a low level for a day or two. Get the hang of it. See how people talk to each other. Add your bit to a conversation here and there and see what happens.

Be personal, but remember you're in public. Don't say things you'll be ashamed of later and don't be mean. You can't really take it back, even if you erase it. Why? Because your enemies (and some of your friends) will have re-tweeted it to the heavens before you can delete it. This is why Tweeting while drunk is a bad idea.

Be transparent. If your Twitter persona is for a corporation or if you're looking for a job, let people know either in your profile or by your tweets. The more open you are about who you are and why you're on Twitter, the better.

Put the flamethrower away. There are certain individuals on Twitter who have become quite high-profile by attacking the social media bigwigs at every opportunity. Do we laugh occasionally? Well, sometimes, but in the end we don't respect them and we don't trust them. Is that who you want to be friends with?

Be open-minded. When you create your new Twitter network of pals, think out of the box. Listen carefully for people talking about things that interest you in other niches. If you only talk about one subject with people, they get bored with you. Branch out. Talk about your hobbies and follow people doing things you always wanted to do. Someday you might get the opportunity to do something through one of your new buddies.

It's Not About You, You, You, Glorious You!

If all you ever talk about is you and how smart, witty and perfectly fabulous you are, we will all turn our backs on you and pretend we never saw you. Share your Tweet-stream with people you admire (if you don't have any, find some). Send out links to blogs, websites or Tweets from people that are just as smart as you. Better yet, even smarter.

Add value. Share information through links. You can't keep all the good stuff to yourself. Share links with a very short and clear description so people know what to expect when they get there. Leave room for somebody else to talk and you'll get more conversations.

Finding People to Follow

I like to keep an eye on who is following the people I enjoy reading about. For example, you've been following somebody who shares a lot of good information and is well respected in your field. Go to her profile and see whom she is following. Are these people you want to engage? Follow a few and then start a discussion. Go see who is following them too—you may find some interesting people. This also helps you grow a niche network among your followers so you're talking about the same things and finding some commonality, as well as getting to know their other interests.

Getting People to Follow You

First of all, be interesting. Share links to blogs, websites and other Tweets that people in your area of interest will find useful.

I find the best way to engage somebody you want to follow you is to listen for a while to see what their interests are and then share some information—a link, an answer to a question or a problem. Don't be put off if they ignore you. Some people set their alerts in Twitter to off so they don't see any tweets to them unless they are following you too.

Automation Is Bad

When people do follow you, don't automatically follow them back. It can be tempting to set up an auto-follow script, but this is a mistake for many reasons. Not the least of which is there are a lot of spammers and bots adding themselves as followers. Follow them and your conversations get clogged up with spam and time wasters. I know it's hard. Especially when you get 10's or even 100's of followers a day, but this is about relationships. If you auto-follow, you could be suddenly following a bunch of people you don't want to talk to and have nothing in common with. Then you have to un-follow them and that takes time.

There's a trend on Twitter to send a message to new followers saying hello and thanks for following. While this can be a good idea, it's been so abused that many people turn the direct message alerts off altogether, and if your direct message thanking them for following doesn't seem sincere, they will un-follow and even block you from getting their updates. Nothing will turn new followers off faster than getting an automated response. If you really do have a kick-ass white paper, tell me in public and I just might re-tweet the link.

Twitter and Search Engines

Twitter can do a lot for building up your personal presence in the search engines and that of the websites you link to. When you post a short URL to a website on Twitter, most (not all) of the URL shortening services can be read by the search engines and so that link now counts as a precious back-link to the site it links to. Get enough of these with the same keywords associated to them and you've got a traffic builder.

If one of the goals of your Twitter presence is to drive traffic to your blog, website, whatever, then you want to carefully craft your Tweets to be most effective. Do your homework and build a keyword list around the topic you want to rank high in the search engines. Make sure these keywords are in your bio. (It still has to sound like natural language; a string of keywords is a waste of time.)

When you post a tweet, make those first words in the Tweet really count. That's where you want to put the topic and a keyword. On Google, you've got about 42 characters for the title in the Google search results. Make sure your tweet sounds like a good descriptive title in those first 42 characters.

When you shorten URLs, make sure the shortening service you use is going to be read by Google. Bit.ly and Tiny URL are good for this.

Don't point all the links to your own site. If your goal is SEO, you want your profile to rank high as well as the site you want to promote. So use those keywords when you have conversations too. Maybe you don't want to use them every time you link to a competitor's site, but remember that what you're trying to do is associate your name and website with the keywords.

In addition, make your site or your blog Twitter friendly. Add a link to Tweet your blog posts or share information on your website and let other people help you drive that traffic and generate interest.

Guy Kawasaki uses an application called TwitterHawk to watch for Tweets related to the categories of blogs listed on Alltop and then send them a Tweet telling them about it. (Say you tweet you were into archery, Alltop Tweets you and reminds you they have a site called archery.alltop.com.) Pretty cool, but probably best if used in moderation. People like the personal touch, not the auto message.

Facebook

Facebook is another network that takes some warming up to, and I will be the first one to tell you that not every business needs a Facebook page. There are lots of people who will tell you I'm wrong. They'll probably also tell you they can build you one for a low, low price. Why? Because anybody can build a Facebook page. There is no real skill involved in building Facebook pages. What it takes is understanding their convoluted system. Once you've got that down, it's a piece of cake. Well, then they'll change it, but you can learn the ropes again.

So don't pay big bucks to get your Facebook fan page built. What you *might* either pay for or learn (hopefully from this book) is how to use that page to grow your visibility, establish your brand and your reputation using Facebook as one of your tools.

While it's true that Facebook is the largest network of its kind in the world and is growing at an amazing rate, that doesn't mean it's perfect for your business.

Facebook is great for touching base with your long lost school friends, posting your family pictures or participating in one of the many groups on a personal level, but therein lies the problem with Facebook. It's entirely too personal. You can create a profile on Facebook and post only your professional information. You can create a group for your business and a fan club for your products. What you can't really do is effectively control where it goes from there.

If people "friend" you or join your group, you're opening the door to their profiles and their friends' profiles and you'd be amazed what people post out there. Before you know it, you and your market can be knee deep in invitations to hook up, embarrassing videos and pictures of friends and loved ones or people you don't even know, and a host of invitations to time-sucking games and vampire battles. Employers have used the network to do background checks on potential employees.

Virgin Atlantic fired a group of service attendants for their discussions on their Facebook group even though Virgin has their own Facebook page for the company. The employees were not following company policy and they paid for it.

I'm not saying there isn't a place for Facebook in your social media plan. I've got a profile and I have thrown a sheep and had a werewolf fight or two myself. What I AM saying is that Facebook is not where I go to connect or collaborate professionally.

In addition, with the advent of Facebook Connect, the new web-wide sign-in system, pretty much anything you or your friends do online becomes shareable data.

Okay, so when IS Facebook good for business?

There are cases where Facebook worked beautifully for a business. Dean Koontz built both a Facebook and MySpace profile for a character in his book 'Odd Thomas;' the two sites quickly became fan sites and fairly effective for sales of the book, complete with fan testimonials.

Many wineries and restaurants are using the site to create fan clubs or hold contests for their customers. Software companies like Serena software built private groups for their employees to use as an intranet for its 800 employees instead of installing custom software.

Apps that play on the fun aspects of Facebook have been a big success. Facebook's iPhone App had over 1 million users in just a couple of months after the launch. Other popular apps "sell" for a few dollars, but the number of users quickly translates to big bucks.

Visa created the "Visa Business Network" app, which takes information about users to help them better network with other small business owners. They also worked with Facebook to offer those that install the app a credit towards advertising on Facebook.

Facebook polls are a wonderful way to reach a large market and sample their opinions, IF the people taking the poll are in your market.

So, the bottom line?

I know there are those who say Facebook is the be-all end-all for business. The fact is, it's not for all businesses. The people who tell you it's a necessity may mean it's a necessity for them. They'd love to build you a Facebook page. It's one of the easiest things you can do on a network, yet people make a living doing it for you.

Before you decide to go there, take a good long look at what you want to accomplish and what your options are. If Facebook is a good fit for you, great; if not, don't lose any sleep over it.

Some people like to keep Facebook just for their friends and family. It's more of a personal experience and they don't want to invite people outside of their circle to join. That's okay. If you still want a Facebook page it's easy enough to set up a Fan page (or several) for your business. People who fan the business page are not connected to your profile, and if they ask, you can politely decline the invitation.

Others use their Facebook page as sort of a closed network of close business associates or teams. Again, just set up a fan page if you really think you need one.

So how do you decide if Facebook is right for you? Here are a few questions to ask yourself.

Do you have a product or service that has a natural fan base? Will people talk about it, and more importantly, talk to each other on your page about the product or service you offer? For example, Facebook is great for books (there's a Facebook page for this book), bands, organizations and causes. There are Facebook pages for Coke, Pepsi, Skittles and Pizza Hut.

What's your risk tolerance? Crazy things happen on Facebook. It's a brave business that allows people to post freely on their wall and share their friends' updates too. You'd be amazed at the insane things people do and say on Facebook. Either be ready to watch it or turn off the Superwall, and make sure you read the Facebook privacy policy so you're aware of what the rules are.

Are the people you want to engage active on Facebook? This is a toughie. Just because they have accounts doesn't mean they want to talk to you on Facebook. You might think that if there aren't already Facebook groups around your area of interest it's not a good fit, but Facebook is changing. Businesses really are finding ways to make it useful, so just because there aren't pages or groups in your area of interest doesn't mean it won't work. You could break new ground. Before you dive in and start building pages and groups, do a little polling to find out if your target market is interested.

Do you have the bandwidth? Facebook, like all social media venues, takes some maintenance. You can set up alerts to keep an eye on it, but you really need to actively seek out members to build your page's fan base. What's your plan for this and do you have the time to do it? Especially in the early stages, it's important to find ways to drive traffic to your Fan page. If there's nobody there or there are no discussions, then people who do find it don't want to be the first.

Okay, so you decided it's a good fit. Here are some promotion ideas to bring more fans to your page.

Link to your new Fan page from all your other social networks. Send it out in your newsletter, put it in your email signature, and add it to marketing materials.

Run a focused fan building campaign. Contests work well for this. Make sure they have to post a comment or participate in some way and not just join. The more the interaction, the richer the experience and the more likely they'll come back. Maybe they can post videos or images that relate to your product? Stories of their own experiences, Q&A sessions, etc., all work well.

If you are building around a service, you could set up regular times when you'll be online to answer questions. Say every Wednesday from 1–2 PM PST you will answer all questions. Then the answers and interaction are archived right there on your site for future users.

If you have the option to build a game or Facebook app that directly relates, that's great. These applications aren't as expensive to build as you might think, and can really create interest. If you want to get some ideas take a look at the thousands of apps and games that exist. Maybe one could be adapted to what you want to do? Generally the developers of these games are happy to re-cycle some code and put a different twist on it.

Building a Facebook Page

I'm going to lay this out at a very basic level so you can see the concepts. I'm not going to give it to you step by step because the steps will have changed by the time this is published.

Pretty much anybody can build a Facebook page in 15 minutes or less. Actually there's nothing to building the page at all, and don't let anybody tell you different. If you're on Facebook now, you're probably already familiar with all the tools available, so why not build it yourself?

I've heard outrageous quotes of as much as $1500 to build a page on Facebook, and the really amazing part is that is all they would do for that sum. Creating community or training on how to use Facebook as a business tool was extra. This just makes me nuts. So here I'm going to show you how to build your own Facebook page for free and how to enrich it and make it a useful tool.

Log in to your Facebook account. Scroll down to the bottom of the page and select Advertising.

Yes, I know this makes no sense, you didn't think you wanted to build an ad, but bear with me here.

At the top of the advertising page you'll see a link to pages. Click it and when you get to the "Pages" page, click the link to create pages. (This is where you will manage your pages once you've built them.)

This next part is the most important part of building Facebook pages. You'll get a screen where you decide how you want your new Facebook page to be categorized in their system. **Important:** Take some time to think about this to make sure your page shows up in the categories people will be looking for you or your services. Just like SEO keywords, a mis-categorized page doesn't get found by people who would be interested in what you have to say. Once you select your category you won't be able to change it again.

Remember, you can have as many pages as you want, each with their own function. Maybe one is a fan page, one for your business, one where you focus on a particular product with a link to buy it, etc. You may want to create two pages with slightly different categories to see which performs better.

Local, Brand or Product

You have the option to create a local page, which is great for businesses that offer local services like restaurants, galleries, services, etc., or to create a page for a brand or product. Click the radio button for each and explore your options a little if you're not sure which category to use. I'm promoting my website so I've chosen Brand or Product and selected Website. Enter the name of your Facebook page. Remember, once you create this you can't change it, so think about keywords as well as the name of the site and the titles in the HTML page you're promoting. You can't change this once you publish the page.

Click create page and that's it, you're done! Okay, well not done, but the page is built. See? Piece of pie.

Now you're ready to dress your new Facebook page up a bit. Again, I'm assuming you have some familiarity with Facebook already, but even if you don't, you should be able to log in and follow along. Since the re-design, Facebook pages operate even more like a profile, so it should look pretty familiar. A couple of additional items on pages are quite useful.

Applications

There are exactly 6 bazillion and 3 apps for Facebook pages. What you want to put up depends entirely on what you are interested in. Do some searches for things you're interested in and scan the apps to see what's there. I know you'll find something. Apps are a good way to add content, but more importantly, to give your fans a way to bond with you more deeply. If they use the same apps as you do, you're already sharing, and new content gets added to your page without you having to come up with everything on your own.

One caveat about apps. Think before you install. Does this app reflect the nature and corporate culture of your business or your personal goals? Is there any possibility the app could offend the people you want to connect to? No? Cool. Go for it.

Custom apps

If you have the skills or the funds, this is a good place to spend some of that money you've saved. Create custom apps like games and dynamic content that will set you apart from everybody else and draw people to your page.

Custom Tabs

Probably one of the most exciting things in the new Facebook design is the ability to create custom tabs and link directly into them instead of the default. This means you can direct people to specific promotions, events or ads you want them to see right when they reach the page. Handled carefully, these inbound links can convert a lot of new visitors to fans and friends quickly. Why dump all your users into a page full of updates when you can direct them to specific information that interests them? This is particularly useful if you're running a promotion or an ad. Just link the ad to a tab until it's no longer needed and then delete it.

Content, content, content

It's really great that the news feed feature is now pretty close to real time and you can bring in feeds to add to your content, but don't stop there. Add unique content your users can only find here. Post Q&A sessions, videos, games or other content that will be its own draw to your page. If all of your content comes from your FriendFeed stream, why wouldn't they just go there instead?

Don't dump it all up there at once. Portion out a few nice tidbits at a time. This will make it easier for your friends to absorb all the great content and let you pace yourself a little.

Events

Events are a great way to reach out to your friends and extended network and grow your fan base. Post your events on your page and let people RSVP and invite their friends right on Facebook.

Tagging

Post videos and photos and tag other users in them. If you host an event, post the pictures for everybody to share with their friends. This is a great way to reach out of your own network through the networks of the friends tagged in the pictures or videos.

Admins

If more than one person will be adding information on a regular basis, you have the option of adding them as an admin. Click "Add Admins" and select a friend to help with the page. (The person must be a Facebook friend already, or you can friend them and do this step later.) The person will get a notification in their inbox and will have to accept it to become an admin on your page.

Suggest to Friends

Suggest your new page to your friends to help you spread the word. It's a good idea to get your content into the page before you start sharing it with your friends and advertising it. I usually wait to publish the page until I think it's got enough content to be interesting.

Profile it

Now that you've got a spiffy page with amazing content and fans are starting to see it, make sure you tell people beyond your friend network about it on Facebook. Put it in your email signature, in your personal profiles on other networks. Add a link on your website and promote it through your newsletter. Any communications you send out should show this info as well.

Become your own best fan

It's a good idea to be your own fan, but again, wait until you're ready to show it off to the world before you fan your page. Then tell all your friends and invite them to your new page!

Add the Fan Box to your website

The Facebook Fan Box is a snippet of Java Script that will pull the latest friends and posts right onto your website. You can put it on your blog and ask your fans if they want to put it on their site too!

Patience

Sooooo you did all the work, you faithfully upload content on a regular basis, but where are the cheering hordes? You may have to give it a little time. Facebook popularity can be an amazingly quixotic thing. No one really knows what's going to flash and what isn't. If you've got good content and you make the page something people will find fun and useful and share with each other, you'll see your fan base grow. Give it a chance.

If all else fails

Think about running an ad on Facebook or even Google to show the page off outside of your network. Ask for opinions on the page from people who aren't going to gloss over the bad bits and act on that feedback.

Flickr

Flickr is often thought to be just a place where you share family reunion photos or some blackmail pics from spring break. It can be so much more. Have you got a new Powerpoint demonstrating the highlights of your product? Pull the most interesting slides and save them on Flickr. People may be looking for a company logo or information about your product and this is going to show up on Flickr when they do a search. Heck, if the slide is really good, they may quote you or use it in their own presentation or a book. (That's how I found that slide on Motrin Moms from Jeremiah Owyang.)

Think of Flickr as a place to show off your best graphs and graphics.

12 LinkedIn

People tell me all the time that they only use LinkedIn as a contact management site where they keep the links to business connections and little else. Wow, way to miss an opportunity.

LinkedIn is an amazing resource for and to information and it's really easy to establish yourself as a resource to boot.

As with all networks, you need to set up your public face before you dive in, and LinkedIn has a lot of tools to give you ways to let people know who you are and what you stand for.

Start with your profile. Upload a business-friendly picture; fill out the forms about your personal and business history. Remember, recruiters use this site a lot, so speak to them and potential connections in a businesslike manner, but give them a reason to read beyond the first few lines of your profile.

LinkedIn is crawled by the search engines too, so get some good keywords in the description tags, but don't make it too obvious. Make a special effort to write a well-crafted summary of what you do. This should cover your skills and strong points so someone looking to hire you or connect with you sees a clear value in connecting.

Once you've got this set up, go to contacts and add connections. You can enter a list of emails or just one and send invitations, import your email contacts, search for colleagues and classmates based on the profile information you shared, or do a search for specific people to connect with. LinkedIn will send an email to your connections with a link to your profile and ask if they want to connect. They can accept or just ignore you as they wish.

If someone doesn't connect after a few weeks, it's okay to either contact them by other means or retract your invitation. Some people rarely respond to these emails or check their accounts, so they may have just missed the connection.

When you've got a few connections, you can ask one or two at a time to recommend you on LinkedIn. This sends a message to them that they are special and important to you, connects you more deeply on the network and lets the connections of both parties know that this person recommends you. It is quite common to reciprocate or to recommend someone first with the hope they will recommend you back. Just like on other networks, these recommendations are part of the criteria for deciding if you want to connect with someone. They also can mean a lot for your personal reputation.

When a recommendation is received you see a copy of it before it becomes public and you have the opportunity to request changes if something is inaccurate or mis-stated. If it's all good, make it public and your network as well as the network of the person who made the rec-ommendation will be notified.

LinkedIn has a lot of applications to help you promote yourself. Import your visual CV, slides from Slideshare, your blog RSS feed and several others. Browse the tools and see which work best for you.

Groups. There are several reasons to join LinkedIn groups. Meet and converse with other business people interested in the same topics. Establish your own reputation as a resource for information. Locate and connect with other people in your fields of interest.

Just as with other groups and forums, share information, ask and answer questions. Be helpful, accurate and friendly.

LinkedIn also has a section called Questions and Answers. This came before groups were added and allows you to ask and answer questions on a variety of topics. Other users can nominate you as an expert or recommend you to the person asking a question. This can be a valuable way to get in front of the people you want to connect with.

There are several different "open Networker" groups on LinkedIn, and while they are a useful resource to go to and find people you're interested in, going the 'add and accept all comers' route can quickly lead to inbox overloaded with spam. So choose wisely who you connect with.

13 FriendFeed

FriendFeed just gets more interesting every day. Some may say it's too hard to use or it should have more or less features, but you have to look at FriendFeed for what its purpose is. FriendFeed was initially a place where you could bring your social network RSS feeds into one place and share your information and your favorite links with your friends and see theirs too. FriendFeed helps you share your stuff, discover the stuff your friends think is cool and discuss how cool it is. Seems simple, doesn't it?

Soon after FriendFeed launched, people started forming "rooms" where they could focus on sharing around areas of interest and broaden their network by meeting other people with similar interests and sharing and discussing with them too.

Social media took off and suddenly there were a LOT of social networks that you could feed into your FriendFeed page. You can bring in micro-blogs, videos, blogs and all kinds of other content as well as your own thoughts for discussion. People can "like" what you post and/or comment on it and there are often spirited discussions around the topic from a wide range of people.

All of this can seem a bit overwhelming to a newbie to social media, but if you start slow and follow a few easy guidelines, you may find you use FriendFeed as a central repository for your social media information.

Setting up your FriendFeed page

Like all social media networks, you want to start with your home page. Add an image, fill out your bio and add some of the RSS feeds to your other networks, if you have them, by clicking the add services link. Don't feel like you have to put them all up right away, you can add more later. You might want to think a bit about which of your profiles you want to be your core and open for discussion. You can also link to the RSS feeds of feed readers like Google Reader or Netvibes and share your favorite feeds through FriendFeed.

You'll also want to set up your email and IM settings. You can get daily or up-to-the-minute alerts when you get new "subscribers" or someone comments on your post.

Now that that's out of the way, do some searches for keywords you are interested in, names of people you'd like to connect with, organizations or brands you'd like to hear about, or email addresses of people you'd like to invite to join you.

Okay, so now you've got a bunch of fascinating information flowing into your FriendFeed page. It's likely you're overwhelmed by just how much of it there is. Don't panic. There are tools to help stem the tide and make it easier to browse.

Lists

When you first sign up, all your incoming feeds go into your home feed. Here you can quickly scan the most recent news and respond, and you can have as many lists as you want.

You can have as many lists as you want. I create one for friends, family, top posters and for each of the different areas of interest. I also have a sort of "A List" for clients and people I want to make sure I don't miss.

Filters

Sometimes somebody is live blogging an event or on a rant about something on one of the services and swamping your feed with stuff you just aren't interested in. You don't have to stop following them. Just set a filter to hide the info from that person for a while. You can also hide particular feeds, though I'm not sure why you'd want to do that.

Now let's say you are fascinated by a new application and you want to hear everything that comes through FriendFeed about it. Do a search for it (iPhone app) and create a new list of all the people talking about it.

Groups (aka Rooms)

FriendFeed rooms recently changed to being called groups, but you'll still hear references to both. These groups have a lot of uses. They can be just for fun, to talk about particular areas of interest, for groups of organizations to talk among themselves. You can choose to make your group private and decide if you want people to be able to vote or comment on things.

If you set up public rooms, you accept a certain level of responsibility to keep them populated with interesting people and information for them to discuss. You have to feed the conversations or the room goes quiet and nobody comes there anymore. If you moderate this well, people will look to you as a resource and hey, you'll BE a resource. Cool, huh?

Being a good FriendFeed citizen

Do I have to repeat, at this point, that it's not about you? Sure, you want your personality and your opinions to come through, but if you really want to be a good community member, you need to support others as well. Before you post a link to a blog post you just read, do a quick search and see if somebody else has already started the discussion. If there's a lot of buzz out there about the latest iPhone app, why create a new thread? Simply comment and share that post with your network.

Give credit where credit is due. If somebody tips you off to a good post, or a feed you really got excited about, tell him or her thanks on FriendFeed. Link to one of their posts on FriendFeed, their blog or even another social media site to spread the love.

Don't leave the conversation lying there waiting for you to respond. If you post something and get a lot of responses to it, you might want to add your own thoughts to keep the conversation going. It's not always going to go on forever, but it may be they're thinking you've left the building.

Support somebody else's position with data if you have it, or bring it to the attention of somebody who does. The idea here is to facilitate conversation as well as to participate.

Remember that just like all your other networks FriendFeed can lend a hand in SEO too. Post links to new information on your blog, your other feeds and other files that mention you or your brand, but don't over do it. This is about building relationships through sharing and that's a two-way thing. Share your links. Share other people's links. Connect with people who have like interests. Discuss topics that interest you. Repeat.

14 Video

Most people immediately think of YouTube when they think of video online, and why not? The site is hugely popular with more videos posted there than any other site in the world. But so what? People also think of YouTube as the biggest time suck in the world, even more so than Twitter. How are you going to make it something you can sell to the CXOs and still be interesting?

Start with ease of use. Sites like YouTube, Seesmic, Vimeo and others make it super easy for you to upload a video and distribute it in just a few minutes to thousands of people. You can create your own "channels" to distribute videos around a particular topic or theme and quite quickly find your following, drive traffic to your website and build buzz about your product.

That doesn't mean you have to be stupid or silly to make a splash. Sometimes simple is best.

Take the videos from a group called Common Craft. The videos they turn out are deceptively simple in design and concept, yet one of the most effective ad campaigns ever. Simple to understand, yet cool can't be beat.

Maybe you've got a new product or method to demonstrate. Do it with a video and share that video on your other social networks. Get it shared and you're on the way to building buzz.

Are you able to do a video demonstrating a process or your skill set? How about a video presentation about how you see your market changing or opportunities? You could do a video resume and post it on YouTube, Seesmic or Vimeo. If it's appropriate, do a series on 12seconds.tv with industry tips and tricks, then post a widget full of them on your blog.

When David Moye was laid off from his job as a writer, he decided to follow his passion and transition into PR. He'd done a lot of consulting, and for some major firms like Hill & Knowlton, Fleishman Hillard and Edelman, but he knew his lack of agency experience would make it tough to break into a new career. He also knew he had to find a way to stand out in a hurry. Being a creative guy, with a deep understanding of the principles of PR, he grabbed his daughter's hand puppets and started a YouTube channel called PR Puppet Theatre. He used the puppets to teach concepts of PR in a way that any one could understand.

Being a savvy PR guy, he marketed PR Puppet Theatre to TV stations and posted and commented on blogs related to the industry. He set up LinkedIn, Twitter and Facebook profiles to help build the buzz and give prospective employers a way to learn more about him.

CNBC saw it and dubbed it "must-see entertainment/education for every PR flack."

Before long, he had interviews and then a job at the PR firm, Alternative Strategies, where he quickly showed he could make the transition. In a few short months on the job, he single-handedly broke standing records for TV placements that had previously been set by a team.

"Facebook is good for someone like me who is trying to make a name as a creative. A few quirky comments here and there (plus a good photo) and I have peripheral friends commenting with me and that's how friendships develop." – David Moye

What's the Lesson?

David didn't wait around for somebody to ask him for an interview. He made some noise all on his own and showed that he had what it takes to get noticed. Isn't that what a PR guy does?

When it's your turn, take the initiative to be daring. Take some chances and strut your strong points. Then ask for what you want clearly and definitely.

Keep videos short and sweet

When you're thinking about videos for web distribution, think short. Try for 1–3 minutes maximum to deliver your message. It's better to break it up into several short pieces and **distribute** them separately, thereby increasing the number of links back and forth and crating something new for users to come back to again and again.

Speaking of SEO, YouTube offers several ways to tell the world what your movie is about. Title, description, tags, ratings and comments all affect your Google rank as well as your visibility. Think carefully when setting this up for maximum distribution. Then share links to your networks and watch your traffic grow.

How-to videos are a huge way to get traffic and they don't have to be on a product you own. Many consultants have built their business on how-to videos of products they want to get hired to work with.

Video services

I love Vimeo for its high quality videos and the TV-like quality, but it's not really appropriate for how-to and quick webcam videos.

Seesmic excels at personality rich snapshots. And it's really great for quick video captures of a moment, a technique tip or even comments on your blog.

12SecondTV is a lot harder than it sounds actually, but if you can think of a series of short videos, only 12 seconds in length, you can deliver a lot of bang for your time spent.

Bottom line, whichever video service you use:

- Think of how you can get the word out about your videos.

- Include videos in blog posts, emails, Tweets.

- Put a clickable link in the first line of your description (under 25 characters).

- Comment on videos on the channel with a link to see one of yours or a **relevant** bit of info on your blog or website.

- Create a video in response to a video you've seen. This is wildly popular and offers wonderful traffic-generating capabilities. Just be respectful of the original poster, please.

- Don't forget your call to action. Don't leave a possible lead not knowing what to do next!

- Build an icon or banner that goes on all your videos. Keep your brand front and center, especially in case the video is shared or embedded on other sites.

- Use YouTube's insight feature to find out which videos are performing well, and then think about why and how you can do even better next time.

Whenever I think of video and social media, I think of Robert Scoble. This blogger/author/photographer started interviewing people for Microsoft's Channel 9 video team and he clearly understood from the start that in order to be in on the cutting edge he needed to be available and create an amazing network of resources to information—both to help him find information and to share what he was doing with the world.

His blog was already popular and he put his contact info (even his cell phone number) right on his site so anybody with a story could contact him to have it covered.

In 2006, he left Microsoft and joined PodTech, where his "Scoble Show" really took off to rave reviews. Everything he was doing, from back stage shots to interviews, was documented and shared, and his popularity went through the roof.

In early 2008, Scoble left Podtech for FastCompany, where he had two shows, FastCompany Live and ScobelizerTV. He's now working for RackSpace on Building 43, a content and social networking website.

So what's the point? Big deal, Scoble is famous. He's a MEME, for godsakes. There's even a unit of measurement for social media success based on his achievements.

A "milliscoble" as definded by followcost.com is: "1/1000th of the average daily Twitter status updates by Robert Scoble as of 10:09 CST September 25, 2008."

In 2008, Scoble averaged 21.21 tweets per day, so a milliscoble is 0.02121 tweets per day. Anybody with a milliscoble rating of 1000 will be as annoying to follow as Scoble.

Something to aspire to? Perhaps. I never find Scoble's Tweeting annoying, and I've found some amazing resources, some entertaining interviews and some good connections through his work.

What's the lesson?

The point is his videos were always timely, mostly useful and never over produced. We forgive the fact the camera angle is funky or there is a lot of background noise when he interviews at a conference because it's REAL. Scoble opened doors with his personality and his camera lens and he got people to talk to him.

Chapter

15 Blogging

Blogs (short for web logs) started out as online updates and diaries. Bloggers posted their thoughts and shared them with their friends, posted progress on a new project, or documented the birth and growth of their baby. It didn't take long before writers and journalists picked up the idea and soon we were reading posts from the thought leaders in all kinds of areas as well as product reviews and citizen journalists documenting news from the streets. In 1989, there weren't many bloggers in China to document what happened in Tiananmen Square, but by 2006, there were over 30 million bloggers in China.

In 2009, when the Iran elections were hotly contested, blogging and micro-blogging were the only way to get the news from the street out to the world. Protesters rallied to many forms of social media to get their message out and be heard. In fact the US government asked Twitter to delay a scheduled update that would interrupt the flow of information through the popular service.

Blogs are pretty interesting and you don't even have to blog yourself to get a lot of value from them. Once you know how to find them, you'll find blogs on just about any topic you can think of and there's sure to be one that will interest you. I scan hundreds of blogs each morning, looking for ideas to bring to my readers on the various networks or to share with my clients that pertain specifically to their businesses.

Okay, I know that sounds like a load of work again, but really it only takes a few minutes to scan the headlines for titles that catch my eye and decide which ones to follow up on.

Remember to make the titles of your blog posts keyword-rich but intriguing, so when they show up in an RSS feed people will want to click on them.

Where do I find all these posts? Believe me, it didn't happen all at once. I've been collecting blogs for years. At first I created an HTML page with links to all of them. That was in the days before RSS feeds and each blog had to be visited every day to see what was new. Painful.

RSS feeds came into being and life got a lot easier. **RSS** stands for **R**eally **S**imple **S**yndication (it also used to mean Rich Site Summary) and it's widely used for websites, blogs, bookmarking sites, life-stream aggregators and community sites to distribute information. RSS was created by a company called Userland, in the late 1990's, and the RSS we know today was formalized into what is now called RSS 2.0 by Dave Winer—one of the forefathers of blogging—in 2002, when he worked with Userland.

All of this is just background though, what you really care about is that RSS feeds allow you to get information when a new post is made in the form of the title, a link to the post and a short description of what it's about. You can get RSS feeds delivered by email, import them onto a page for easy distribution or read them in a reader where you can add feeds that catch your fancy, scan the titles or simply read the posts. right in your reader.

There are a lot of options to read your RSS feeds, but once you get a lot of feeds to read, you need to find a tool you're comfortable with to manage your feeds.

Google Reader is a popular feed reader and you can add new feeds easily right from your web browser.

Chapter

16 | Creating Your Social Network

Don't put all your eggs in one basket.

Social media trends come and go in the blink of an eye and nobody wants to get caught putting all of their marketing efforts into the wrong network or platform, only to find nobody goes there anymore and all that work is worthless.

Besides the mercurial nature of social networks, there is also SEO to consider. If you have content on a number of sites all talking about your product and pointing to your main presence and contact information online, there are a lot more ways people will be able to find you when they look for that product online.

As a rule of thumb, I think you should have at least a blog, one micro-blog and a presence on one of the major platforms or article sites.

Let's say you're a marketing consultant. You post a new social media press release about the latest trends on your website. Here are a few ways you might quickly promote it:

- Tweet it to your network

- Post an excerpt on Tumblr or Posterous with a link to learn more

- Add a link on your delicious.com, Stumbleupon, or other bookmark pages (carefully tagged)

- Get it posted on SocialMedian.com

- Propose an article on marketingprofs.com

- Write a short post that uses the same keywords but from a different perspective on your blog

- Build a Squidoo lens for the topic

All of these should link to the page you want to highlight, and even better if you can link between a few of them as well to increase your overall visibility.

Creating Profiles

You'd be amazed how many people think profiles are unimportant. These are often the first thing people read to find out about you and your company. If it doesn't give enough information or it's offensive or silly, they may assume that so are you. Always create a full profile before participating on any social network. Build a little file on your computer with a well-written bio, some basic information about you. A couple of headshots or avatars and you can set up your profiles quickly and easily.

See what your company policy says about setting up usernames and mentioning the company in your profile.

Social Bookmarking Sites

Social bookmarking sites are abundant and a very popular way to save your favorites, share them with friends and drive traffic to your content. The most popular are: Digg, Yahoo! Buzz, StumbleUpon, reddit, delicious, kaboodle, Propeller, twine, diigo, blinklist and newsvine.

There's no way I can go deeply into social bookmarking without writing a whole second book, but there are some basic truths to know about social bookmarking sites that can help you get on your way and avoid the biggest mistakes.

Every post, image, multi-media piece, or video you do can be marketed through a social media bookmarking site somewhere. The question is, which one? You need to give a little thought to the goals here. Who is your market and where are they bookmarking?

Do some searches on a network you think you might want to use and see what quality of content comes up. Do you see the same people over and over posting links in your niche? Where else are they posting? How often do they post? Who are they connected to?

How many posts are there of interest to you on this site? Will you be unique or totally alone? Alone isn't good. If you are marketing a recipe site, it may not be a good fit for a bookmarking site that focuses mostly on technology and software like reddit. If your site is all about product reviews, kaboodle is probably a good fit.

You get the idea? Find a few networks that you are going to post on at first—I'd say 2–3 to get to know and find the users you want to connect with. Maybe they are in the same field or maybe they have a complementary interest. Read some of their posts and vote them up, re-share them with your network or otherwise support them, even if you don't have anything bookmarked yet. Start building the relationships first, and then start posting your own links.

Don't ask or expect that they will re-share every single post of yours. Be patient. Quality content gets shared.

How long is this going to take?

We've all heard the stories of the post that made the front page of Digg and instantly rocketed the site to stardom. This is very cool when it happens. It doesn't happen very often. In fact, about 100 users on Digg control more than half of the posts on the home page. They are VERY popular because they can really help you if they want to.

Why would they? If you support them, link back to them on other networks, only bother them with your finest content when you ask for support back and wait patiently, you might get it. Or you might not. All is not lost though. If you keep putting out quality content and supporting other quality content, the users will notice and maybe someday you'll be one of those top 100.

Until then you're going to have to build this castle brick by brick and be patient, friendly and persistent. Here's an example of how that can pay off.

Automation (Yes, Again)

There are a lot of ways to automatically post your links to social book-marking sites with robots, services and the like. Here's the thing. If there's no connection with other users and they just get posted to the site, they just lay there in the hopes someone will stumble across them and re-share. Bookmarks don't really do you any good on their own. It's the sharing and re-sharing that make the buzz build, and get the search engines buzzing too.

Automated posting systems quite frequently are seen as spam. They create fake accounts on a whole host of sites that may not be at all related to what you're interested in and that reduces the value of the links. If you're going to do this, you're going to have to work for it, but your results will be a whole lot better, more focused and solidly based in the future, and that's where the traffic is!

SpliceToday.com is a web magazine that produces unique, off-beat articles on topics ranging from politics, music, sex, sports, and top news stories.

The content is organized into a collection of linked articles, original writing and multimedia.

As you can imagine, this is a tough space to differentiate in, and SpliceToday needed to build their brand and traffic so they could really shine. They worked closely with Prime Visibility, a New York marketing firm, to market individual articles through bookmarking and social media sites and a Facebook ad campaign.

Prime Visibility's social media marketing team marketed each and every article on the site through the appropriate bookmarking sites for the piece based on what the post was about, the target market and the community on the bookmarking site.

Prime Visibility created relationships with other users on these sites for reciprocal sharing, a crucial factor in social bookmark sites. The deeper the relationships with other users, the more likely they are to share your posts with the right networks. The response to the campaign accumulated slowly at first, and then as buzz and reciprocity increased, it really took off. In just 7 months, the combination of Facebook ads and social bookmarking showed dramatic results:

- Increased total visits/month – 3,435%

- Increased total page views/month – 1,922%

- Increased total referring traffic/month – 6,230%

- Increased total unique visitors/month – 4,691%

What's the lesson?

Launching a new site can be painfully slow to get off the ground, unless you really put some elbow grease into it and market every bit of content you have. To do that, you have to carefully analyze the market for the best fit for each piece of content.

In order for social bookmarking to work, you can't just run a bunch of robot scripts and call it done. You have to create relationships with other site users, cross promote and support them, as part of the community to see reciprocity happen.

In addition, setting goals and figuring out how you will measure success is crucial from the get-go so you can see how effective your campaign is.

Chapter 16: Creating Your Social Network

17 Social Media Etiquette

All communities seem to have a lot of unwritten laws on how you behave. It really isn't the wild-wild west that some people think it is. At least not if you want to promote your business.

Most of them are just plain common courtesy while some of them are specific to the platform. What I'm posting here, in no particular order, are the ones I try to remember and I encourage you to add your own for us all to learn from.

Fill out your profile and upload a picture. Before you start engaging on any platform, let people know whom they're listening to. When someone discovers your carefully written and deeply valuable first posts, they're going to come to your profile to learn more and decide if they want to talk to you. If you've got the default icon and no info, they may wait until later. There is no later. They'll forget you.

Don't follow a bazillion people right off the bat. Choose your friends carefully for the value they add to you and your network. You're looking to build relationships, not notches in your cyber bedpost.

Auto-follow is lazy. I know it's harder to maintain a lot of relationships one at a time, but that's actually the point. Taking the time to develop real relationships instead of "Twitter acquaintances" is important to add the most value out of those connections.

Only direct message when absolutely necessary and do not auto DM for any reason. The same holds true for automated private messages. If you can't bother to take the time to personally message me why should I listen to you? Trust me. I won't.

It's important to make sure you check the message you're sending out to your network. Is it of a person who shares good information freely and encourages and supports others in their network?

Is your public persona one that you would respect and want to know (if you didn't already)?

While it's important to share, and sometimes to be the first to share important news to build your authority, don't forget to leave room for somebody else. When commenting or creating a new post on a forum if you say everything there is to say about a subject, no one else gets to talk. You just sucked all the oxygen out of the topic and nobody else can breathe. Instead, try to leave your comment open ended so it encourages others to say more.

When you write a Tweet, make sure there is room for it to get re-tweeted. That means leave at least 20–40 characters at the end, so when someone re-tweets it to their network, they don't have to shorten your Tweet.

Be polite ALL the time. Keep in mind that while you may be perfectly right to call somebody out for a misstatement or even openly taunting you people aren't always going to see it in context. That smart line you threw off in the heat of the moment has to stand by itself if it comes up in a search and there may not be any point of reference for the user who finds it months later. It just makes you look like a jerk.

Instead of biting back let the storm blow over and make a comment that either supports your argument with a link to data or simply let it go. Life is too short to encourage enemies. Then keep an eye on what that person is saying and look for an opportunity to support or engage them on something positive. Don't suck up, just be polite.

It's harder to be nice sometimes, but trust me, it pays off much bigger and not only do others have a better impression of the person you are so do you!

Always thank people for linking to your blog post or mentioning you. It doesn't have to be a reply on the site, it can be a direct message or even an email or a phone call. Let them know you appreciate their time and you heard them. Then make a mental not to see how you can give something back to them down the road. Support them by pointing out a great blog post or make a good mention of them in the media to your network.

Comment a lot. Make it a habit to look for forums, networks and blog posts that interest you—even if they're not related to your business. People want to know something about the person they're talking to as well. So if you fly fish in your off hours, go ahead and comment on somebody's fishing trip. Comment on a business blog only about business. Make sure it's on topic and concise, and again, leave enough for somebody else to talk about it too. You want to stimulate conversation you can participate in, not dominate the room.

Rules of Engagement

I know I've told you it's important to build a network of social media profiles to grow your visibility, deliver your message more broadly and gain more opportunities to learn from your connections, but I do not subscribe to the belief that mega-networks really pay off all by themselves. That said, I had a sort of revelation that changed my mind and helped me see how a large network really could be useful.

I have a couple of monster-networker friends on LinkedIn. I've always sort of pooh-poohed the "LIONs" (LION stands for "LinkedIn Open Networker." These users believe in gathering as many connections as possible.) and the people who had thousands of connections on

LinkedIn as multi-level marketing opportunists who figured the more connections they had, the more likely the spam they kept throwing out would find a home somewhere. So I pretty much avoided connecting with people who had a LION designation or had thousands of followers.

I answered a question on LinkedIn, the person thanked me and asked me to join her network. She's a mega LinkedIn Q&A person, and I could tell from her answers that she gave them some thought and really tried to be helpful. So I connected. Over the last few years I've only gotten helpful posts from her, the occasional newsletter, but she's never once tried to sell me anything. I figured she's a rare exception to the rule, and when I see something I think will be useful in her business, I send her a shout.

We live thousands of miles apart, so we never connected face to face, but we've sort of stayed in touch and whenever there is a LinkedIn event in my 'hood, I often hear about it from her first. That's how I met mega-networker #2. He was holding an event in San Francisco to meet some of his connections and she passed along the invite to her network in the Bay Area. I met some really great people at this networking event, and I learned quite a few things about how a real networker creates both a large network and strong relationships. I watched how he made introductions, then encouraged the others to connect and talk among themselves. The event was not about him. It was about the network.

Your network by itself is only a list of names, job descriptions and resumes. In order to make a humongous network useful, you have to go deeper than just making connections. You have to find out about people and connect to them on a deeper level. You need to find commonality and a way to be useful to each other. Traveling to a conference in a far away town? Take a look at your network and find out who lives there. Where should you eat? What should you do? Do they have time for coffee? Somebody in your network holding an event you wish you could attend? Who else in your network might like to know about it?

Of course, it's likely you'll never meet many of the connections you make face to face unless you attend networking events. How else can you be helpful and a valuable addition to their network? Read their blogs and comment or share the link with your networks. Send them an email about something you think they might not know about. Really take the time to find out who they are and why you're happy to know them. Once you understand what their needs are, start connecting people within your network to each other. You are only the center of your own network from your perspective. Everybody else sees it from a different viewpoint.

All this is to say I finally realize that mega networkers are not necessarily spammers. There truly are people out there who understand the value of relationships and have large networks. So take a moment to think about your networks. Who is adding so much value you can't help but want to share them with the rest of your connections?

What's the lesson?

All mega networkers are not spammers. If all they talk about is their numbers, feel free to ignore them. If they come back to you with answers to your questions, connect you with other users or information, treat them like gold!

18 Managing Groups and Forums

Managing forums and groups on the various networks can be either a lot of fun or a thankless task full of drudgery and conflict. But it doesn't have to be that way at all. The difference is in how you see the groups you are managing. If it's you against them, you're going to hate this job. Go do something else. Find somebody who is a natural evangelist and likes people to do this job.

BUT if what you want to do is find ways to really get people talking about whatever it is the group is for, then you can really have a lot of fun. It's all about attitude.

Focused interest groups can be a powerful way to connect with other business people in a meaningful way. Here are some tips for beginning community managers as well as experienced community managers. Remember, creating the group is only the first step. It won't thrive if you don't nurture it.

Forum (group) management is also known as moderation, and it's a whole lot more than just deleting posts and putting out flame wars.

- The most important thing is to be an active manager. Every registration needs to be manually approved, preferably with a welcome email telling them how they can use the group, interact with you and how to get in touch with you.

- Contact members directly with helpful (not sales) information, on a regular basis.

- Scan LinkedIn and your other networks for likely members and invite them to join or get introductions from members to people they think would be good members.

- When a user becomes prominent as a poster, support and encourage them. These are the catalyst to a thriving group.

- Even if somebody is a bit obstreperous, unless they openly attack someone, they can be good to stimulate the community. Handle them with care and they can turn into evangelists.

Are people continually posting off-topic discussions such as jobs? Give them a place to post those and point them to the jobs board in the group.

Engage

Remember this is about COMMUNITY not YOU. You should participate by all means, but to support the community, not sell yourself or your services.

- As the group grows, think of other ways to connect people. Meetups, tele-classes, webinars and online chat are great options.

- Periodically take the temperature of the group. Poll or ask questions.

- Listen to discussions and see if users are looking for added feature, if there are ways you can offer assistance yourself or point them to assistance off site. The goal is to become a source users rely on, not make the whole show about you.

- In the development stage of the group, or later if discussion slows down, start discussions. These should be open-ended posts to stimulate discussion, not statements.

- Give the users room to add their perspective; don't hog the conversations or always be the first one with a bit of hot news. The group will begin to rely on you and not post for fear of being overshadowed.

- Brainstorm with your key community members within and outside the group to get new ideas flowing.

- Remember to thank people for their participation. Feature people on occasion for their contributions.

Share

- When new features are added to your group's software, share how to use them with the group, ask for success stories and examples.

- Make connections and suggest connections between users, where appropriate.

- Take the time to point out new features and how to use them for best advantage.

- Create a way for users to showcase their talents. Sharing Slide-share presentations, Visual CVs, Job listings, product demos, whatever you can to give your community a voice of their own and sense of ownership in the advancement of the community makes for a healthier, more vibrant membership.

Promote

- Promote your group by sharing it with your networks and ask users to do the same.

- Post the group URL on your website and related social media sites to encourage growth.

- Create a badge or a widget with the most recent posts for users to put on their websites linking to the group.

- Talk about the group and feature conversations (with permission) on your other networks (Twitter, Facebook etc.).

- Use Google, Facebook and LinkedIn ads to promote your group.

- Whenever you do a presentation or attend a conference spread the word about your group.

Have Fun

The whole idea behind starting a group is to create a place where you, your peers and friends learn together and share ideas. Do take the time to enjoy the group and the people in it.

Commenting

You don't have to have a blog, your own forum, a Twitter account or even a Facebook page to participate in social media. You can participate very effectively through commenting on blogs, forums and social media sites. When you find a post that resonates with you, add your thoughts and get in on the conversation. Add value to the conversation. Offer your expertise. Support the poster if you agree with them; and if you don't, be respectful and offer data for your argument.

When participating like this you can quickly become a vital member of the community and a resource to whom people turn to, both on- and offline.

Remember though, this is still a public venue. Be transparent about who you are and try to be consistent. If you go all Jekyll and Hyde, people won't trust you. Did you ever hear somebody say "She's exactly the person I thought she would be?" That's a successful personal brand in action. Remember you represent your brand, especially if that brand is you, and anything you say on social media networks is part of your brand's legacy.

Backtype

If you are a regular commenter and you find new places to post through searches etc., you can find yourself in the odd place of losing track of everywhere you posted a comment. Short of bookmarking and cataloging each one, Backtype keeps track of your comments on blogs and keeps a running list for you. Even better, Backtype allows you to follow other members' comments so you can see what they've said and where they're having discussions and join in too.

Amplify.com

This is a service that lets you clip snippets of websites, blog posts, forums, etc. and then post them to your own account on Amplify, complete with your comments on the clips (and a link back to the original page). The post can be delivered to your Twitter, Facebook or social bookmarking account as well, and commented on by other members as well as your network.

I find Amplify a great tool when I don't want to write an entire blog post but have more to say that will fit comfortably on a micro-blog. The ability to clip a section from a site, with a link back to the original is a real time saver. The site it's clipped from gets a little extra promotion and traffic, and I can create a discussion around their content in just a couple of minutes that can be continued on multiple platforms.

Amplify has a feature that lets you follow other users and see when they clip new posts. This is great because it reminds you to come back to check out the new content, and you can keep on top of what your colleagues are talking about.

Disqus

Disqus not only tracks your comments across sites like Backtype does, it integrates into your own blog to help you manage and gather data on the comments on your site. They've recently introduced a slew of sharing features that can reduce the number of plug-ins you need to install and make it easy to manage from one place.

Chapter
19 Crowd-sourcing

You might think of social media as a great way to get feedback on a product or service, find the best vendor or find out what people think of Flip Mino video cameras before you buy one, but there are much deeper applications. Crowd-sourcing is a way to leverage the knowledge and interests of a large number of people to gain insight, solve problems and create content.

Traditionally when doing market research, the marketing team might locate a few people, bring them into a room with some video cameras or a one-way mirror and ask a bunch of questions. Then they'd gather all the input and evaluate it by hand or type it into a database. Or they might set up a phone bank and make a lot of calls and enter what they get into a database, use mystery shoppers, phone banks, field interviews or surveys.

Social media opens up a raft of new ways to reach potential sources of information through crowd-sourcing. Many sites have popped up to help you reach a large network of people without even having to pester your own networks with piles of questions about every iteration of your product.

Ask500People.com is a very simple site that allows you to ask any question you want of a diverse and de-centralized group of people. Users post a question and it goes into the queue where other users can give their opinion and comment on the question. Instant reporting gives you basic demographics on geographical location, education, gender, age, and income. It's a great way to get consensus on a question quickly from a random group of people and even some feedback.

Ideablob.com allows you to input your great business ideas and have them voted on and gather input from members. Members vote on the worthiness of particular ideas and one per month wins $10,000 to get their idea off the ground. In May 2009, Epic Change was the winner for their idea to invest the $10,000 for a technology lab in a small primary school in Arusha, Tanzania. Epic Change rallied hundreds of people, who may have never used the web before, to cast their votes in Internet cafes across Tanzania, to show them how the Internet could change their lives and the lives of their children in ways they could not have foreseen.

This was not Epic Change's first investment in Tanzania. The organization loaned funds for land and construction to expand the school in December of 2007. In 2008, they loaned another $30,000 (much of which was raised through a Twitter campaign called Tweetsgiving) towards additional construction and a school bus, and then launched a line of products to be offered for sale online, and the school has used those funds to begin to pay back the initial loans. The school has more than doubled in students, and in November 2008, the students sat for the national exams for the first time. The school ranked #1 out of 117 participating schools in the Arusha district.

Ideascale is a crowd-sourcing platform that lets you post questions for feedback from customers, solicit their input and ideas and then have the crowd rank them in importance by voting.

The City of Austin, Tx. used it to get feedback from citizens on the features of the city website, for which they would be using local software developers, marketing experts, and graphic designers displaced from their jobs due to the economic downturn. This, according to the website, "will produce a superior website for the citizens of Austin at a fraction of the cost of the city's lowest bid."

One of the most obvious governmental uses of crowd-sourcing has been President Obama's effort to really hear the voices of the American people. He used several platforms to do this, including Ideascale's platform at opengov.ideascale.com, where the people were allowed to post ideas, discuss and refine others' ideas and vote the best ideas to the top of the pile for consideration. According to their website: "Because of your participation, this dialogue has generated a rich collection of ideas that will shape the President's commitment to making our government more transparent, participatory, and collaborative."

For more examples of governmental use of collaborative efforts and crowd-sourcing, visit the Global Development Commons, an initiative of the US Agency for International Development (USAID), where you can find social networks of all shapes and sizes blossoming, who plan to foster innovation in technology that will promote international development through collaboration.

Local Motors is leading the pack in the automotive industry. The company runs an ongoing contest on their website for environment-friendly auto designs. Users of the site enter competitions to design everything from roadsters and race cars to the interior based on that of a Rally Fighter plane. The company plans to build "micro-factories" where designers can build their concept in a prototype facility and eventually actually drive it home.

What's the lesson?

As you can see, one of the really great things about these collaborative platforms is their ease of use to many and the speed with which they can be put up and start to collect data and ideas. Not only do you not have to have your own engineers, you don't need to host the platforms, and set up time can be extremely fast. With this kind of power behind it, a passionate team of innovators and their collaborators can go far.

Chapter

20 | Non-profits

Grassroots Organizations

Social media channels are perfect for grassroots organizers to quickly create buzz and find their following. Take the case of Help A Mother Out. Lisa Truong and Rachel Fudge saw an Oprah segment on the tent cities outside of Sacramento filled with homeless people with nowhere to go. They were moved to contact local shelters to see how they could help and the shelters told them their biggest need was for diapers and toiletries for babies and children.

Then they discovered that Federal and State safety net organizations that support poor and homeless families do not provide diapers for babies. Federal support funds like WIC and food stamps do not allow the funds they give to be used for buying diapers. This leaves poor mothers in the position of deciding to use what expendable cash they have to buy diapers or food.

So they set out on their own to change things. They contacted their personal network of friends and family. They set up Amazon wish-lists so people could donate funds directly, publicized the lists on their blog and set up several direct drop locations where people could donate.

Although the original target date was for Mother's day, the response was so overwhelming that by the end of May they had collected over 15,000 diapers, as well as thousands of other hygiene items for babies, children and mothers.

Lisa says, "A year ago I was totally anti-social media—Facebook, Twitter, blogs, all that stuff. Once I got on Twitter and started talking about what we were doing, it just took off!"

Now we've got 700 followers and we've connected with so many people across the country that have the same passion as we do. We've seen some far flung friends who saw what we posted and became very closely involved and host drives in San Diego and Santa Clara. A friend in Italy heard about it and got her friends in Tucson to set up a program.

The blog has been good too. People are linking back to us. We got in touch with a couple of good connectors who had bigger networks than we do, and they shared it with their networks."

While on Twitter, Lisa noticed that some Silicon Valley moms were talking to Katie Couric about children in the recession. She picked up on their Twitter hashtag and basically crashed their Twitter conversation to tell them about what Help A Mother Out was doing. Although she never heard from Couric, Kim Tracy Prince picked up on it, and became the Los Angeles co-ordinator for a program there. A producer at KGO radio in San Francisco and a blog post about them on SFAppeal.com brought them onto the show for an interview.

They also started a conversation with a diaper bank in Michigan, and Sally Lieber (a former California assembly member) started a conversation to encourage changes in the way WIC works so they begin to cover diapers.

Help A Mother Out teamed up with a tiny baby shop called Baby Buzz in San Jose's Willow Glen neighborhood for a donation drive. The goal was to bring in 1000 diapers for a local women's shelter. Local bloggers picked it up and blogged and tweeted about it and a local bank (Valley Credit Union) saw it on Twitter, gathered up over 1,000 diapers and the staff delivered them to the shop that very day.

The immediacy of seeing something Tweeted, being able to take action and get immediate satisfaction of helping are very powerful things. Valley Credit staff did a video of the event and posted it on their Facebook page, which was linked to by many supporters of Help A Mother Out as well as people in Valley Credit Union's network and it was a clear win for everyone involved. The store got great publicity and felt good for helping. Help A Mother Out donated the diapers to a family shelter and an Asian women's shelter in San Jose. Valley Credit Union staff got the immediate satisfaction of taking action and helping out as well as positive press as caring members of the community.

"The Help A Mother Out campaign is exactly the kind of grassroots effort that is needed today. Social networking in service of supporting needy mothers is a fabulous idea. Through innovation and utilizing the free tools the Internet has to offer, HAMO has made a big difference to the lives of many women and children, and in such a short period of time."

Danica Remy, President, Point Foundation, Publisher, Whole Earth Magazine & Catalog

What's the lesson?

One of the most powerful things about social media networks is how easy it is to get into a conversation. It was easy for HAMO to stir up interest at a local level with goals that were easy to reach and understand. Yet when they started repeating their efforts over and over, they were able to have a huge impact on the health and well-being of both mothers and their babies.

Start small, be consistent, reward your supporters with praise and thanks, and they will support you back.

There are hundreds such examples of grassroots organizations springing up organically around a simple desire to help. Social media allows them to quickly spread the word to their networks, and if the idea is valid, it's likely to take off very quickly.

Is this the future for non-profits? I think it will be. Raising awareness of a cause is a significant aspect of the mission of most non-profits and that aspect can be as much as 25–30% of their administrative costs.

In a survey of non-profits conducted as part of a study on administrative fundraising by the Center on Philanthropy at Indiana University (2001), 1,542 responses from a nationally representative random sample reported their fundraising costs were 24 cents per dollar raised.

One of the requirements of a 501(c)(3) organization is that the donations come from a broad spectrum of donors, which means resources need to be dedicated to finding those donors, and historically that's been an expensive process. Flyers have to be designed and mailed, press releases have to be sent, advertising in magazines, on radio and TV need to be produced and often at least partially paid for. Even if the non-profit opts for email instead of newsletters and marketing, pay-to-play email systems cost plenty in their own right.

Social media allows organizations to leverage the networks of their supporters to reach much further than by traditional means. Not only can they use it to raise awareness of their cause, they can also use it to fundraise within their networks and those of their supporters, giving them a much broader reach for a lower overall cost.

There are online fundraising services available that cater to a non-profit's needs. Some offer integration with forums so the organization can create community around their mission and use the community itself to help get the word out and bring donors to the site. Some facilitate fundraising by offering ways to donate through unconventional means like cause fundraising on Facebook or services like Tipjoy that accept donations right through Twitter.

Because of the current economy, options like this are very attractive to donors as well. They feel like active participants in the cause and seem to get a much larger sense of ownership on the organization because they are able to actively interact with the organization through the online presence. If something needs to get out quickly to the masses, it's a simple thing to rally the troops on their various networks and send them out with a strong message. This use of a donor's networks to extend the reach of the organization's own network is a very powerful thing.

Support Organizations

Non-profit support organizations like TechSoup and their NetSquared initiative specialize in helping non-profits get the technical knowledge and help they need to succeed online. They offer forums and an abundance of ways to use social media effectively through meetings online and offline.

charity: water

charity: water is one of my favorite examples of fund and awareness raising through social media. Here I'm using it as a best case scenario, and even a tiny non-profit can use some of these techniques to improve their awareness and fundraising efforts.

In 2004, Scott Harrison traveled to Liberia with a humanitarian organization called Mercy Ships which offered free medical care around the world. In that trip he photographed the doctors and patients and became intimately aware of the urgent need for the most basic necessities. In 2006, he founded charity: water, an organization whose mission is to provide clean water to the over 1 billion people who don't have access to it. They do this by drilling wells, setting up filtration systems and water holding facilities. All of the funds raised by charity: water goes directly to water project costs.

How do they do it?

charity: water really is an amazing example of how to use multiple social media avenues to reach different audiences simultaneously. The message is stated clearly on all their marketing materials.

"charity: water is a non-profit initiative bringing clean, safe drinking water to people in developing nations. For $20, we can give one person clean, safe drinking water for 20 years."

They have a strong online video component and a large database of images and videos available on their site so that journalists and bloggers can easily access the information they need to help spread the word. The first thing they did when they finished their first projects was to upload the pictures to tell the story of what they were trying to do. This kind of quality photography and content really makes it easy for a blogger to do her job, and if it's easy to write, the story is more likely to get published.

Their press kit is a downloadable zip file chock full of information, quotable data and hi-res images so a journalist can quickly pull together an informative and visually impactful piece. They even offer links to Google maps to show where water projects are underway.

I won't go into detail on the dozen or so networks charity: water is active on. You can get the full list on their website at charitywater.org, but let's look at the highlights.

charity: water's YouTube channel is full of videos of water projects underway and the people they serve. In addition, there are videos from people like the Budde family who helped to raise enough money to build a well in Ethiopia. These videos are compelling, easy to share and all end with a simple call to action. The YouTube videos alone have been viewed over 1 million times.

charity: water has a good following on Twitter, and at least part of that is due to Amanda Rose and a small group of fellow Twitter users who met at a Tweetup in London, UK to raise money for a local charity. They got to talking about how they could raise more through Twitter, and within two weeks, they'd decided to host a virtual festival (a Twestival) to raise money for charity: water, spreading the word through Twitter. Twestival took off and spread across the globe. All in all, more than 200 cities around the world held simultaneous Twestivals to raise over $250,000 for a total of 55 water projects in 3 countries.

The organization also makes good use of Facebook's "causes" appli-cation which allows friends of the page to donate directly on the site and then notify their friends of the cause and the donation. This kind of social pressure works quite well, in fact charity: water raised almost $1 per member on their Facebook page through this kind of donation.

They've also used a social networking site called SocialVibe for effective fundraising. This site encourages users to select up to two causes or charities to support and then be "sponsored" by their favorite brands. The user posts a badge on their public profiles with the sponsor's logo and the more times the profile is visited the more is donated to the charity selected by the user. As of the end of 2008, SocialVibe raised over $200,000 for causes and charities worldwide.

What's the lesson?

Well, the first and most obvious is that social media is a good way to raise awareness and funds quickly by leveraging the networks of people who believe in your cause. The key is to find people who are good advocates and have a large enough sphere of influence to really help your efforts get off the ground. Sure you can create a Twitter account, a great message and encourage your entire network to spread the word, but unless your network contains people with influential networks of their own it's going to be a slow start.

Go back to that chapter on listening and start identifying who can help you reach more people and get those conversations going. Listen to their ideas and input too. If we've learned anything from events like Twestival, it's that what seems like a small idea can take off like wildfire if the right influencers get engaged.

Social guilt is a big deal. When one of your friends donates on Facebook they can tell all their friends. If their friends don't donate too, they feel just a bit guilty, but if they do, they get to add a note or a badge to their site and let all their friends know they donated. It sort of becomes a contest to see who can convert the most friends and generate the most for the cause. Social guilt is your friend.

Make it compelling and make it easy to share. High-quality YouTube videos are easy to share with friends, and are also easy to embed on a blog post touting your message. Make images, video, soundbytes and quotes very easy for bloggers, journalists and your supporters to find and use to help spread the word.

If you're on Twitter, set up a hashtag to track everything about your organization or a particular event. This makes it easy to track what's being said and easy for someone to pull it all up in one place and write a story about it.

Keep it short. Fundraising through social media has performed better with smaller goals and short time periods. Twestival was only two weeks long. That's about as long as people care to "listen" to the tweets about the event and are willing to re-tweet it to their friends. Keep the message very focused, raise the money quickly, report how much is being raised in real time if possible, then take a break and re-group. If you're constantly chattering about the next event, people may tune you out.

Post often and at varying times. People are busy and they may have simply missed your last micro-blog post. Don't slam them with tons of posts, but don't be afraid to post a few times. This is especially true if there is a deadline looming. "Only 1 more day. We only need $1,000 more" is effective. Lots of people wait until the last moment. Don't give them a chance to say "I meant to and then the drive was over." Tell them it's ending!

Don't get stuck on one channel. All of these different networks exist because people are different. People who spend time on MySpace may not be at all interested in Facebook. Some prefer forums or Ning groups to any other network. Others are only on Twitter. Spread the love around a little and then watch carefully to see which networks work the best for you. You may end up dropping some or promoting others to the top of your list. You may also find that there's a certain synergy between two or three networks that helps them all grow.

Talk back. On any of these networks simply broadcasting your message and making it easy to see is only a small part of the strategy. You have to talk back to the people involved in your community and engage them on whatever level you possibly can. Listen to their ideas and suggestions. Answer their questions. All of this re-enforces the message and you never know where a brilliant idea is going to come from. Give your supporters a sense of ownership in the organization and the knowledge that you appreciate them, and they will trudge a lot farther in service than you they you might think.

Set up a corporate policy. This is essential when you have a team of volunteer management to work with. You can't have them clipping the logo from a web or misquoting you. You want to give them guidelines so they keep the standards of all communications about your cause on target.

Working with Volunteers

Use your volunteer force. If you can get your causes' supporters to start tweeting and talking about you in forums and on social networks with links back to your site, it can be a huge traffic driver. Encourage them to do this. Hold training sessions on how to use social media to empower them. Post a page on your website just for supporters with information they can use, and logos and excerpts from your corporate policy so they get the terminology and credits right.

Build community with your donors and supporters. Take the time to notice people who go above and beyond for the cause. Feature them in a blog post or just say thank you on Twitter. Their network will appreciate your recognition. They may even blog about it. Remember that they CHOSE to support your cause. Give something back to them for all they do for you.

Look for networks for non-profit organizations. There are several good resources for non-profit organizations online where you can learn more about social media networks and techniques that work. I really like what they're doing at netsquared.org. They're showing organizations how to use social media networks and tools to build community and generate interest, and their forums are chock full of good resources and advice. You should also look into the Non-profit Technology Network (nten.org) which also has loads of good research information, resources and an annual conference on non-profit technology.

Chapter

21 | Measurement

Only you can determine what it will take to prove your efforts are a success. So what will it take?

Measuring engagement can be a tricky process. For example, BusinessWeek has a tool they call the "Reader Engagement Index," that basically calculates the ratio of comments to posts on their blogs. Okay, that measures the engagement on their blogs, but if a reader simply reads a post and forwards the link to a friend, quotes it in their blog or encourages one of their connections to comment, then these numbers are skewed. If they do all or most of those things, the numbers are WAY off.

Forrester Research defines the engagement between individuals and brands in terms of the four I's: Involvement, Interaction, Intimacy, and Influence. How do you measure that?

Well, maybe you can.

For small business owners ROI on any investment is crucially important, and it can make jumping into social media pretty scary because of the lack of hard numbers.

So often when I present on social media somebody in the room wants metrics to gauge the success of the campaign. The question about metrics is, what data would be valuable to you and how do we measure it accurately? Of course, you can measure the increase in traffic, the number of comments and links to your blog, the number of users and posts in a forum, how many views of a podcast. But how does that translate to sales? Do those metrics tell you the value of your campaign?

We gotta do what we gotta do, and many of us who work in social media have gone to great lengths to either create or locate our own systems for gathering metrics on social media ROI. I use a combination of tools depending on the client, the most important things that need to be tracked for them, and which platforms they're implementing. Getting that balance right and finding as much as we can about a particular niche is getting easier every day. We've come a long way from reading raw server log files and field interviews to learn about whether it's working or not.

Chapter

22 Efficiency Matters

I've run into several people over the last few weeks who are taking breaks from some of their social media networks because of input overload.

It starts simply. Following a few links you found on Twitter, then the blogs you're reading have really great links and the sites at the end of those links have really cool videos and then you get lost in YouTube for an hour wandering down a trail of videos that quickly change from being fact-filled and data-laden to silly and funny and completely worthless, but now your brain is so fried you just don't care.

That's usually when your boss or a client calls and you cannot form a complete sentence in response to their vitally important question. No amount of explaining will get you out of the hole you're in, so you blame it on sleep deprivation (without telling them you were posting videos on Seesmic all night) and promise to be bright-eyed and bushy-tailed at the meeting in an hour. That's the one with the proposal you were supposed to be writing while you were watching pointless but beautifully-filmed Vimeo videos or playing Spymaster.

I'm pretty sure this has happened at least once to every social media contact I have. I refuse to disclose how many times it has happened to me.

There is a way to survive this phenomenon and gain back at least a smidgeon of your productivity. It's called scheduling. There is no earthly reason you have to have Facebook, Twitter, Google Reader and FriendFeed open 24/7. Missing a post by an hour or two or even (gasp) six will not destroy your business (unless you're doing customer support on these networks).

- Set up a schedule you can live with. Stick to it and you'll suddenly have lots of free time in your workday for those mundane but necessary tasks.

- Read RSS feeds in the morning before you get to work. I read mine on the treadmill, but you can download them to your Kindle and read them on the train, or use an RSS reader for your iPhone. Share a couple of links with your network to get them thinking for the day.

- Check your Twitter stream 3–4 times a day—in the morning, coffee break, lunch and at the end of your WORK day.

- The rest of the day, rely on notifications and alerts to let you know when you need to respond to someone.

- Figure out the times the people you want to engage with are usually online and let that guide when you log on. (Use your listening tools to see when your traffic spikes on Twitter, etc.)

- Set up reminders to ping you when you get a direct message or a reply on Twitter.

- Set up listening tools to alert you of mentions of you or your brand.

- Create an email address that lands all of your notifications in one email box and then check it every couple of hours. Rome will not burn if a comment doesn't get responded to in a couple of hours.

- Missed a post and you think it's too late to respond? Try email. You can make your response longer and richer. You might even try the telephone.

Now, I'm not saying this will work for everybody, but give it a try and see how to customize it to work for you. You might be surprised to see you can be connected and productive at the same time.

23 This Is Not the End. It's the Beginning.

It took me a lot longer to pull this book together than I thought it would. Why? Because at every turn I see new networks and tools popping up like daisies and it's my first inclination to check them out and see if they should go into this book. This was very nearly an unwieldy tome of lists of networks you just gotta see and tools you gotta try. If I left your favorites out, I'm sorry, and I'd love it if you'd share them with me on my networks, my blog or by email.

As I re-read this book and edited it, I realized that I need to leave a lot of things out so as not to overwhelm you with information. What I've given you here is the core of a good social media strategy. It's a get-started guide, a launch-pad intended to get you started and help you see the promise that I do in community, relationship building and social media.

I have a LOT more to say, and I expect there will be another book down the road that goes deeper, but hey, you can always read my blog at JanetFouts.com.

Keep an eye out too for my next big project. I'm planning on launching something really big that will make it a whole lot easier to keep on top of the latest tools, networks and techniques.

Thank you for reading this book. I hope you'll find it useful and connect with me to give me your feedback—positive or negative, it all helps me fine tune what I do.

Resources

I've mentioned a lot of great resources in this book. Rather than list them all here and risk them being out-dated or broken, I've posted them on my blog:
http://www.janetfouts.com/social-media-success.
Please take time to visit these pages. There are some wonderful resources there and I'll add more as I find them.

About the Author

Janet Fouts is a social media coach, educator and speaker. She helps individuals and corporations of all sizes understand how to use social media tools and work efficiently in this emerging field, and conducts in-house workshops and virtual training sessions on social media tools and strategy in industries ranging from wine and landscaping to non-profits and high-tech companies.

Janet has been working with small businesses to develop their online presence and also with online community for 13 years as senior partner in the award winning web design and development firm, Tatu Digital Media (TatuDigital.com).

Her own personal experience in restaurants, hotels, web development and tech start-ups gives her unique insight into a range of industries.

She freely shares her knowledge on several social media platforms, including her blog at JanetFouts.com and on Twitter as @jfouts.

Janet gets offline by riding the roller coaster in Santa Cruz with her family, hiking, horseback riding, taking the dogs to the beach, wine tasting all over northern California and frequent trips to San Francisco to enjoy walking the city and the cuisine from street carts to fine dining.

RELATED LINKS:

Janet's Blog: http://www.janetfouts.com

Tatu Digital Media: http://www.tatudigital.com

Twitter: http://www.twitter.com/jfouts

Linkedin: http://www.linkedin.com/in/janetfouts

Facebook for this book:
http://www.facebook.com/socialmediasuccessbook

Other Happy About® Books

Purchase these books at Happy About http://happyabout.info or at other online and physical bookstores.

18 Rules of Community Engagement

This book is a definitive guide for those seeking to facilitate and grow online communities and develop social media strategies for themselves or their organizations.

Paperback $19.95
eBook $14.95

Networking Online—Making LinkedIn Work for you!

This book explains the benefits of using LinkedIn and recommends best practices so that you can get the most out of it.

Paperback:$19.95
eBook: $14.95

I NEED A KILLER
PRESS RELEASE
Now What???

A GUIDE TO ONLINE PR

NEWS

JANET MEINERS THAELER
FOREWORD BY ANITA CAMPBELL

HappyAbout.info

I Need a Killer Press Release -- Now What???

If you are a small to mid-size business owner who wants to understand online news promotion, or work for a PR firm who wants to add online optimization and SEO to your press releases, this book is written for you.

Paperback $19.95
eBook $14.95

of Social Media for
Small Business

JENNIFER L. JACOBSON
FOREWORD BY JORY DES JARDINS

42 Rules of Social Media for Small Business

Written by communications professional Jennifer Jacobson, this book is designed to help working professionals find social media that fits their business and get the most out of their social media presence.

Paperback $19.95
eBook $14.95

LaVergne, TN USA
06 April 2011
223014LV00003B/33/P